ONE COP'S STORY:
A Life Remembered

JOHN H. BRIANT

Chalet Publications
P.O. Box 1154
Old Forge, New York

One Cop's Story: A Life Remembered

First Printing November 1995
Second Printing September 1996
Third Printing September 2001
Fourth Printing April 2004

Graphics and Book Design
by
John D. Mahaffy

ISBN 0-9648327-0-4 (Paperbound)
ISBN 0-9648327-1-2 (Hardcover)

Published by
Chalet Publishing
P.O. Box 1154
Old Forge, New York 13420

DEDICATION

To my wife Margaret, and in loving memory of my parents,
John D. & Marjorie A. Briant.

Best Wishes,

John H. Briant

III

Contents

FOREWORD

At this stage of my life I have been able to write this humble autobiography for the purpose of sharing some thoughts and memories of my life gone by. I have been honored to serve the citizens of New York State.

The young men and women entering the State Police Service in the '90's will have a difficult challenge in this complex society. It is my hope that the following pages will show that if one can weather the storm, public service in this organization can be a most rewarding experience.

While this is a true account of my life and my career with the New York State Police and the Bureau of Criminal Investigation (BCI), some names have been changed or deleted to protect the individuals and their families.

Other books by the Author
Adirondack Detective 2000
Adirondack Detective Returns 2002
Adirondack Detective III 2004

JHB

ACKNOWLEDGMENTS

I wish to extend thanks to John D. Mahaffy for "steering the ship", "Rapid" Rick Carman for "harbor navigation", Katharyn Howd Machan for her editing skills, and of course my wife Margaret for her patience, understanding, insight and opinion.

I

Childhood

I

I suppose instant publicity would have burdened my shoulders if I had been born of royalty or from a family of fortune. Why would you even care to read about the memories of a hard-nosed state cop? I didn't have to pull out my service revolver in a shoot'em up episode where blood spills and stains the pavement of a highway or floor of a building. The majority of my encounters consisted of one on one situations. Some of them were packed full of suspense and tension, which goes along with being a cop, but let's not get ahead of the facts. I'll turn now to the beginning of these memories.

I was born in a small northern New York State Village, to modest parents. Mother was from a farm family and father, a World War I veteran, operated a gasoline station. It was April 7, 1930 when my stork swooped in for a landing. It left a seven pound four ounce baby. I am sure that this bundle of joy received plenty of cuddling and love that is so important in infancy. I have always felt and known the love from my parents.

At about two and a half years of age I stuck a screwdriver into an electrical outlet and was more than aware of the electricity pulsating through my small body. There were the bumps and bruises, the spills on the tricycle, and the snowballs that crashed into my body, thrown by the older kids in the neighborhood. There was plenty of love from aunts, uncles and cousins. I remember the first pony ride and the visit to the zoo where the tigers raged and the snakes hissed.

During this time my brother arrived. I can remember mother

changing his diapers, and all those important things like baths, pressing baby clothes, playing with wooden blocks and even more love from the parents, aunts and uncles and cousins. Plenty of loving I remember, so important to a child.

Now at the age of eighty-eight my mother slowly moves her wheelchair through the hallways of a Central New York elder care facility. She gives the appearance of a queen going through her castle with the grace of royalty. Her deep-set blue eyes seek out another lady of her vintage and their ensuing conversation is about another time and place.

The time is in the mid-twenties and the place is the George Timmerman family farm in northern New York State called Perch lake. Mother fills her stories with reflections of her thirteen member nuclear family and their life on the farm. She tells about the handsome horses that once filled the twelve stables of the barn and all the other animals that live on farms. Her story at eighty-eight focuses on the horses with names of "Ben" and "Tilly".

Mother's audiences are the elderly like herself, who listen with interest, but only for a fleeting moment in time, for these listeners are waiting for their final journey.

With the energy of her youthful mind she continues to tell her listeners about the fireplaces filled with beech logs that snap, crackle and pop. Her account of the passing of dishes heaped with freshly popped popcorn mixed with a little melted butter stirs her audience, and the attending nurses are asked over and over, "Can we have some popcorn?"

Fragments of other stories try to flow from the tired mind of a queen who once played piano recitals before national audiences with the power of her fingers which are now bent, but still strong.

The shoe factory where mother worked for thirty-plus years helped keep her mind alert and her fingers sure. She worked as a stitcher for eight hours a day. In that sweat shop a stitcher doing piece work often went without a break or lunch in order to meet her daily goal. Yes! the long hours of piano instruction in her youth conditioned her hands for the position of a fancy-edge stitcher.

I visit mother as often as possible. Many times when I enter her eighth-floor room overlooking the winding superhighway below, she will look up from reading the Bible, and our matching blue eyes meet. The smile that gradually grows on her stately face signifies to me that her love for the number one son is still there in the shadows of time. She seems so much at peace with herself.

Sometimes when I enter her room she briskly asks, "Have you heard from David or Joan, son?" Whether I have or not I always let her know that they are well. Probably down deep she feels the sorrow of not hearing from my brother and sister, but her veil is kept cleverly in place, and our conversation drifts in other directions.

Those other directions go back to the late twenties before the Great Depression of the era. The times that Ann (my mother) and John (my father) spent racing side by side down narrow streets with mother behind the wheel of the new Hudson car and father straddling a vintage Indian motorcycle. Many times we discuss who won the challenge. Mother smiles warmly and insists that the outcome of those races will always remain their secret. I take a moment to myself and think, "What if mother won all those feats of the motorcar vs. motorcycle?"

Father was born in 1900 in a small north country town in Jefferson County of New York State. His father, Henry, was a five foot five carpenter, and passed on before I was three years of age. My grandmother Hattie Briant passed away when I was three and a half years old, in 1934. In 1935 my parents made a major move from the north country to Syracuse. We travelled in father's 1934 staked-racked Chevrolet. All the possessions my parents owned were in the rear of the truck. The incident that stands out in my mind is putting my foot into a fresh-baked apple pie that mother had placed on the floor.

Mother, father, brother David and I arrived at our new rented home in Westvale, located just west of Syracuse on Route 5. A small yellow Cape Cod, it set up on a bank overlooking the highway. A small chicken coop was situated in the rear yard. I remember that Route 5 was lined with amber lights that cast a yellowish glow in the nighttime.

Father, in 1937, was an independent trucker. He transported loads of furniture from the South to New York State. On one trip when he was away from home, mother baked an apple pie and set it on the windowsill to cool. As it was cooling, two hands appeared at the window in the kitchen and stole the pie. We never did find out who committed the theft, but guessed that a hobo may have taken it to satisfy his hunger. In that era of time there were a great many unemployed transients moving through the area.

Father went to work for a trucking firm in Auburn, New York and began to drive tractor and trailers, known as semitrailer-outfits today.

Mother entered me into Cherry Road School, and the first day in kindergarten was a big day for me. While at Cherry Road School I learned how to play the xylophone. After I learned how to play "Silent Night" I practiced every night at home under the tutorship of my mother. I finally became accomplished enough to play the carol before an audience of seven hundred people. I can remember being upon the stage at six and a half years old. My hands were sweaty and I began to play. Out in the audience my brother was sitting on mother's lap. All of a sudden I heard his voice call, "Look it, Mommy, there's brother Jackie!" It was all I could do to continue playing, but somehow I got through it.

When David entered kindergarten at Cherry Road School, we used to walk to and from school each weekday. Mother always cautioned us to hold hands while we were walking. Tony the Cop was always on the corner of Parsons Drive and he would keep an eye on us. I remember him saying to David and me on several occasions, "You Briant kids behave yourself, or I'll cut your ears off!" We knew that he wouldn't do that to us. All the kids loved Tony the Cop, a Town of Geddes Policeman. The children who crossed Parsons Drive in the mid-thirties would remember Tony. He was a special friend to all of us.

In l938 Mother and Father moved us again. It wasn't far away. We moved to Amboy, New York and father rented one side of an old farmhouse. David and I both entered the Amboy School, which consisted of kindergarten through sixth grade.

There was a pond on our rental property, and we spent many warm days in the summer wading. We used to roll old tires around the yard pretending that they were trucks. Father suspended a couple of the tires from a large drooping willow tree and many of our minutes were spent swinging in those old tires. The faster we swung, the farther we went out over the pond.

The day that father brought twelve baby ducks home was a joyful one. We would feed the ducks in the morning and they soon followed us all over the property. We cried terribly one day when one of them we called "Fluffy" went out into the roadway and was run over by a passing car.

A really terrifying moment occurred one evening while we were at the dinner table. David choked on a chicken bone and father had to drive him to Dr. Whitely's office in Jordan, and just in the nick of time. Dr. Whitely saved my brother's life. We were all appreciative to God, Dr. Whitely and father.

While we lived in the Amboy home we had the privilege of seeing the DC-3 Airliners come in for a landing at the Amboy airport. They flew directly over the house, and what a noise they made!

Mother sent David and me to buy a gallon of milk twice a week. It was a mile each way, and sometimes we would stop at Gerald Strickland's home to have hot chocolate and cookies with Dick and Wendy Strickland. They were a wonderful family and watched out for us when we walked to the dairy store.

We did not have very much opportunity to visit our relatives in the north country of New York State. Father seemed to have worked at least six days a week with the Auburn trucking firm. When he did have a day off he would try to take David and me fishing. Sometimes we would come home with a pail of sunfish, and father would prepare them for dinner. Mother would prepare oven fried potatoes and a salad. What a feast! The sunfish were sweet, and father would brag about his culinary skills.

It was a very sad day when my mother received word that her father had passed away in a nursing home near Watertown, New York. Father was on the road with the truck. Mother took David and me to the funeral. The trip to Watertown in our 1934 Ford Sedan took about two hours. I remember a sign at the gas station where mother purchased some gasoline. The sign read, "8 gallons for a $1.00."

Grandfather, George Timmerman was 72 years of age when he passed away. I was only eight years old at the time. He looked so peaceful in his casket. The flowers and cards were very nice. There was a great deal of crying and everyone seemed to have a handkerchief in their hand. It was late when we returned to Amboy that evening. Mother grieved openly for several weeks. It was a sad time for all of us.

In the late summer of 1939 we moved to a small house located in Throopsville, New York, part of the Port Byron Central School District.

It was a happy time, even though there was not very much money coming into the household. Mother and father planted a large garden, and

David and I had the job of doing the weeding. The garden produced a variety of vegetables and mother did a lot of canning. We had a cool cellar, and at the end of the summer the shelves were full of canned goods.

Mother took us to Port Byron in early September of 1939. David entered second grade and I entered fourth grade. The Port Byron Central School was large. It had a student population of approximately seven hundred students from K thru 12th grade. The students were all country kids. The first pupil I met was Harold Applebee. Harold and I got along fine. We rode school bus number three and our driver was Mr. Glen Derby, a veteran of World War I. Mr. Derby was a good driver and took good care of his bus and the students who rode it. He was very strict, but fair.

I became very ill in 1940, with Streptococcus infection. I was hospitalized for a month and almost died. Our family doctor conducted an investigation and learned that the raw milk we purchased at a local farm had become contaminated from a laceration on the hand of a farm worker who milked the cows.

Vividly, I remember one particular day of my hospital stay. The five doctors standing around my hospital bed scared me. They were all wearing white medical masks. I was in horrible pain and was being treated with a sulfur compound. It reacted and my body broke out with a severe rash, which itched and itched. I overheard one of the doctors say, "I think we'll have to operate." Another stated, "Well, before we operate, let us try a two quart oil enema." It was a terrible experience and I don't wish it on anyone. The two quart enema worked and I didn't have to be operated on. However, I missed a full two months of school, because I spent a month home after being discharged from the hospital to avoid rheumatic fever. A person is extremely weak after this type of sickness. The health department talked with the farmer about his hired man. Our family had learned a good lesson the hard way. We never purchased raw milk again.

When David and I got home from school each night there were chores to do. We were assigned dusting jobs around the house. We took care of our small lawn and spent hours in the garden.

Discipline was always present in our household. Mother was the strict disciplinarian. Father was the negotiator. Fortunately for us we learned right from wrong at a very early age. The cardinal rule was followed closely: One thing you didn't do was talk back to your parents.

They were good parents. Now that I'm much older I can appreciate just how difficult parenting must have been during that era. I consider my brother and me fortunate to have been raised in those times.

In the summer of 1941 I overheard mother tell father, "John, I'm ready to go to the hospital." Father arose hurriedly, dressed, and raced downstairs and out the back door to the garage. Soon he had the car backed up to the rear door of the house. Father called a neighbor, Mrs. BarrRelle, who came over and took my brother and me to her house. Father hurriedly left for the hospital with mother sitting in the rear seat of the family car.

It was the next morning, July 12, 1941, when David and I were officially told that we had a sister and her name was Joan Diane, weighing in at seven pounds, three ounces. Boy! Were we excited! Now there were three children.

With a new baby sister our home was a busy place. David and I assisted mother and watched over Joan Diane with brotherly love.

The tires were still being rolled in the driveway, and we also began riding bicycles, first in our yard and then—more adventurously— on the narrow macadam two-lane road in front of the house. It was always a challenge even in those days, because of neighbors going to and returning from work in Auburn. We lived in the valley between two rather steep hills; therefore, much caution had to be taken when we pedaled near the crests of each hill. We kept as far to the right as we could get, a safety measure.

Sandlot softball was popular in Throopsville, and a lot was set aside by a charitable neighbor for this particular activity. After playing sandlot softball for two hours, three or four times a week in the evening, it was sleep time for all the kids. In order to play ball, it was required that before the game, David and I must complete our assigned school homework.

Sailing crude home-made boats in a small creek behind the house was another activity that all the children in the neighborhood enjoyed. The boats consisted of several pieces of wood nailed together. This provided us with hours of enjoyment.

During the wintertime in our preteen days, we built large snow forts where many a snowball skirmish took place. Catching a hard-thrown snowball in the face was a terrifying experience. When we came home after such fierce exchanges, mother would be standing by with a change of clothes and a mug of hot chocolate.

There were several radio programs that our family listened to. One evening when we were tuned into the Gene Autry program. I remember it well: December 7, 1941. At about 6:30 P.M. a special news broadcast interrupted the show and announced to the country that the Japanese had attacked Pearl Harbor. Mother, who was nearby began to cry.

The United States became involved in World War II. The "Winds of War" raged throughout Europe and the Pacific Theater. Mass production took place and the weapons of war, along with legions of patriotic Americans helped defeat the despots.

It was in 1942 when our family moved to another small hamlet, Montezuma, which was, on the edge of the muck lands. Acres and acres of black soil stretched between Montezuma and Savannah. I had no idea that in a short period of time I would find myself working in these eighty rod sections of black earth, from which tons and tons of vegetables are harvested each year.

It was a thrilling experience for us to ride to school on another bus with a different driver than Glen Derby. Floyd Denman was a soft-spoken gentleman and expected the children riding his bus #6 to behave themselves and keep the noise down. We complied, but I caused a stir one morning on the way to school. A big kid kept picking on a smaller boy, pulling at his shirt and causing the little boy to cry. The big bully was wearing glasses, but I jumped up and punched him directly in the nose. Mr. Denman stopped the bus. I knew that I was in trouble. Mr. Denman said, "Both of you boys come to the front of the bus and sit in the seat behind me. I want to keep an eye on you both." The big bully and I complied, and when we got to school we were both taken to the principal's office.

When I entered Mr. Arthur A. Gates's office my knees were knocking. The bully was sitting in the waiting room.

"Sit down in that chair," the principal commanded. I complied.

"John Briant I want you to tell me about the incident on the school bus this morning. Mr. Denman has informed me that you struck a fellow student."

My knees were shaking. I struggled to answer.

"Mr. Gates, sir, I could not stand by and watch Glenn picking on

Jimmy. He was pulling on his shirt and slapping his face."

Mr. Gates slowly approached my chair and stopped about two foot from me. He wasn't smiling. My knees shook.

"John, I have taken the liberty of contacting your parents."

"Yes, Sir," I replied.

"John, Glenn has informed me that you broke his glasses." Mr. Gates's voice was firm.

"Yes, Mr. Gates, I did. I know what I did was wrong, but I couldn't stand to see him picking on Jimmy."

I was thinking all the time, What will my mother and father do to me when I get home from school? My hands started to perspire and I felt as though I were about to cry. Somehow I held my tears back.

Mr. Gates's booming voice continued, "John Briant, you will have to pay for Glenn's glasses."

"Yes, I will," I replied.

"John, you are excused to go to your class, and I might caution you. I do not want to see you in this office again for these reasons. Do you understand me?"

"Yes, Mr. Gates, I understand."

"You are excused, John."

As I left the office I knew that Mr. Gates was displeased with my actions. But he must have forgiven me, for I received Christmas cards each year from him until his death at the age of ninety.

When I got off the school bus that night and walked slowly to the side entrance of our house, I shuddered to think what was in store for me.

"Hello, mom," I said dejectedly.

Mother didn't answer me right away. I walked past her and went to my bedroom. I had not been in my bedroom for two minutes, when I heard mother coming down the hall. I sat in my chair by my desk, and again my knees started to shake and I felt weak all over.

I looked up, and there it was in my mother's hand, the thick brown army belt with the large brass buckle.

The sting and pain were real. The welts were reddish brown and I knew that I was punished for something that I thought was right. I lay on my bed and sobbed for a long time. Ann's German ancestry had struck hard on my back side.

When father arrived home from work that evening I could

overhear them talking in the kitchen. Father did not speak to me all that evening, and I remained in my room.

In the weeks that followed, the exchange of conversation between my parents and myself was minimal. The glasses cost $26.00 to replace, which was paid to Glenn through Mr. Gates's office. The glares from the bully continued till the end of the school year. But little Jimmy thanked me for helping him on the school bus that eventful morning. It had taken me several weeks of cleaning neighbor's lawns to earn the money for the glasses. Although the relationship between Glenn and me was strained, he never sought revenge.

The United States was at war, and gasoline rationing began. Red Stamps were issued for grocery products. Families began hanging stars in their windows to show that a member of their family was in one of the armed forces. Air raid drills were initiated, and all the students at Port Byron Central were assigned homes in the Village of Port Byron in the event of an attack. We would go to these homes during practice drills. The Civilian Defense Corps was established, and I signed up to be a messenger. I was given a flashing arm band to denote my position.

The end of 1942 brought a change of occupation for my father. He was now employed by the Federal Government at Seneca Ordinance Depot outside of Waterloo, New York. A part of their security force, Father wore a uniform to work and carried a revolver.

When Father wasn't on duty, he worked another job to help make ends meet. With his 16 mm sound projector and speakers he would go to all the surrounding towns and show sound movies.

Father used to get his films from the Buffalo Film Exchange in the city of that name. They would come by Greyhound bus. The people in all the small towns of the area enjoyed the movies. This was long before the concept of the open drive-in theater became a reality.

The price of attending, if I remember correctly, was about fifty-five cents. Two of the movies I especially remember were Rin Tin Tin and Sergeant Preston of the Yukon.

He showed movies of Bill Boyd in a cowboy film and Yankee Doodle Dandy starring James Cagney and many others.

One movie showing was on the Onondaga Indian Reservation located just south of Syracuse. The movie was about the RCMP and the Indians of Canada. There were scenes of Indians battling the red-coated mounties. The Indians watching the movies got so excited that they jumped upon the tables of the hall and gave war whoops that curdled my blood. They were wonderful people and respected my father a great deal.

During World War II the families of the area would gather on each other's porches during the evening and discuss the war, the children, and hopes for the future, and grieve about the loved ones lost in battle.

It was a severely trying time. Women joined the work force in manufacturing plants to fill in for the men who went off to war. Every family experienced hardships. In our family we also felt the sacrifice. Mother went to work for a shoe manufacturing concern in Auburn. Little did she realize then, that it would be a span of thirty years before she would return to her home life again.

While mother and father were involved in the war effort on the home front, David and I continued to attend school and do our chores at home, such as preparing the evening meal to assist our parents, who were working all day. It was a team effort, as for most American families.

The years between 1942 and 1945 for David and me were a period of time for schooling, helping out around the home we lived in, and working on the muck lands on weekends. Some of the chores that occupied our muck-working era included weeding rows of carrots, onions and potatoes. Some of the weeding was accomplished by pulling weeds by hand and the use of a hand cultivator. During work days of intense heat and sun, we wore large straw hats or bandanas wrapped around our forehead.

The work day on the muck was usually from seven o'clock in the morning to five-thirty in the afternoon. The wage earned was sixty cents per hour: for a ten hour day, six dollars. The harvest season was figured differently. For example, in the harvest of potatoes and carrots, the usual crate fee would be ten cents. If a person topped a hundred crates of carrots, (fast work!) he or she would receive ten dollars for that day's work. After this kind of piece work a person returned home at the end of the day exhausted.

Father would come to our bedroom at five-thirty every morning and knock on the door and state, "It is time to arise, my sons." I can remember a time that we didn't get out of bed at his direction. We soon found ourselves on the floor, along with our mattresses. This happened on only one occasion. For the rest of the vacation time and until the time we left the family nest, we arose when father beckoned us to do so. He had been a World War I Infantry soldier and a motorcycle dispatch rider, and was a firm believer that children should follow the "suggestions" of parents. We didn't argue with father, or mother.

In 1944, father left his government post at Seneca Ordinance and transferred to Sampson Naval Base until the end of World War II. In 1945 he retired from Government service. He remained a special operative for Dana Detective Agency of Ithaca, New York, where he conducted confidential investigations. I was never privy to the content of his assignments.

The birth of Aunt Sarah's Fried Cakes occurred at the beginning of 1946. A long-time-ago vision came true! When father had been stationed in France in World War I he had come across an old recipe on how to make fried cakes out of potatoes. Through much experimentation for several years in the family kitchen, he created a delicious product. To this day I do not know the exact ingredient content of an Aunt Sarah's Potato Fried Cake, but what I will never forget is the soft texture and the full flavor.

The packages of two fried cakes each were well known in Central New York and the North Country. They first appeared in his shop in Clyde, New York in the later part of 1946. In 1947 he moved to Auburn, next to Kidd's Meat Market, on East Genesee Street. A sign of a baker holding a fried cake was displayed in the front window of the shop. Father's working staff consisted of three people including my sister, Joan.

In 1957, father sold his business after having a heart attack. It was a sad day for him as he turned the keys over to the new owner. I have never tasted a better fried cake than my father's creation.

The vision that I made real in 1946, when I was 16, was the achievement of obtaining my Junior Operator Driving License. I had been driving in fields or the family yard since I was eleven years of age, and bicycles didn't seem so important anymore. After studying the driver's manual I took my oral and driver's test in Auburn. I passed. Boy! did I feel like a big shot!

Father asked "Are you fully aware of your responsibilities now that you have your license?" "Yes, I am," I replied.

Father never had to ask me again. We had only one car in the family in 1946, and it was a special privilege to drive occasionally.

My high school schedule had been planned while in junior high. It included all the mathematics that high school offered at that time, with the exception of calculus, which was not taught. It included all the sciences except chemistry, which I opted not to take. The plan called for three years of mechanical drawing and one year of blueprint reading.

History, English, choir, gym, football and etiquette class were also included. The courses that I took were considered necessary for college entrance. My plan was to attend Oswego State Teacher's College for their industrial arts program and Driver's Education Training.

My brother David was promoted to the freshman year of high school from sixth grade, and I had the privilege of going through high school with him in my class of 1948.

At the time the guidance teacher felt that David, thirteen when he entered the freshman class, would be able to handle the high school curriculum. Both of us would graduate in 1948.

Some of my summer and part-time employment during my high school days included selling The Saturday Evening Post, trimming around the tombstones in the Throopsville Cemetery, serving customers as a Soda Jerk at Marian Margaret's Ice Cream in Auburn, and grinding metal at Henry and Allen Tool Company. Other positions included truck driver at Maloney Lumber Company, laborer for Rochester Concrete Company, laborer for Jackson Perkins Rose Gardens, and harvester at numerous muck farms in the area.

The management took time to explain to the employee what was expected of them. The experiences I encountered in these part-time positions with the various companies and farms did much to shape my maturity and growth. Indeed they are some of my fondest memories.

During my junior year of high school I joined Company I of the 108th Infantry, 27th Infantry Division of the New York National Guard located at the Armory in Auburn. The drills were scheduled for every Tuesday evening, some weekends at the rifle range in Throopsville, and two weeks at Camp Drum, known today as Fort Drum, located in northern New York State.

The military experience was most beneficial for me. Discipline is good for everyone; it helps teach a person to stand on their feet not only physically, but mentally as well. The class instruction and the physical exercise helps mold good character.

The experience on the rifle range acquainted us with the British .303 Enfield rifle, the Garrand .30 Caliber rifle and other military equipment which makes up an Infantry squad, platoon, battalion and division.

Participation in the two-week exercises at Camp Drum afforded the units time to actually experience mock combat exercises. I was a member of the 27th Division for a period of three years and two months. I was honorably discharged in 1950 in order to enter the United States Air Force during the Korean War.

In 1947 Father began construction of our family home located about three miles north of Auburn. The lot was approximately one acre. He created the plans for the house; a two-story structure made of ten inch wooden clapboards, painted white on the exterior.

My brother and I assisted with the digging of the cellar and worked on the roof. Father did the majority of the work.

We moved into the house in the summer of 1948. Our new dwelling consisted of one bath, a large living room, a dining room, a kitchen, a utility room, one bedroom downstairs and two bedrooms upstairs. The garage was attached to the house. The floors were hardwood. It was the place we called home.

There were neighbors to the west of us and across the road, but an open field stretched to the east of the house. Father planted seven poplar trees in the rear yard, and over the years mother was noted for her beautiful red roses that, I must say, had long thorns.

Father loved to look out his french windows and view the roses and shrubbery. His time was divided between the fried cake shop and home. Father occasionally participated in confidential investigations with the Ithaca Detective Agency, but terminated this work in 1955, as the fried cake shop demanded more of his attention.

In June of 1948 at the auditorium of the Port Byron Central School, forty-two graduates in our caps and gowns sat in chairs positioned in a semi-circle on the stage. Mr. Arthur A. Gates, yes, (the same high school principal!) stood before us and the audience.

Mr. Gates's baritone voice announced, "Graduates of the Class of 1948, parents, family, friends and faculty, we are gathered here this evening for a special event." He continued, "It gives me great pleasure to present as evidence of their efforts for twelve years, the diplomas that they so richly have earned at this plateau of education." I looked over at David, who was sitting next to me.

One at a time we got up and advanced toward Mr. Gates. He gave us each a firm handshake and said, "Congratulations." It was an emotional experience for me, and I am sure that my fellow graduates felt the same.

After the diplomas were given to the graduates, the audience applauded for ten minutes.

The graduation party was a gala affair. It was held at the home of Robert McNamara, one of our graduates. The punch quenched the thirst of all forty-two of us. There were all kinds of salads, fruit, sandwiches and party gifts for everyone, celebrating that four hours ago we had received our diplomas.

The party concluded at approximately one a.m., and after thanking our gracious hosts we left the McNamara residence for our homes, where our parents would be waiting. Some of us would meet again at alumni banquets. It actually was the finale of the Class of 1948. Memories of these fellow students still return occasionally: the quips in class, the laughter, the sad times when we lost a sports event, the gossip, the rumors, the good times, and the good teachers that we were so fortunate to have during that twelve years of the learning experience.

(Mr. and Mrs. Arthur Gates have both passed away, leaving behind a legacy that will be difficult to surpass by their replacements. They helped to shape every student who graduated from Port Byron Central School. We give eternal thanks to you, Arthur and Regina, wherever you are.)

Father and mother were standing in the window when David and I pulled the 1941 Dodge sedan into the yard at Turnpike Road, from our graduation party. After father checked the car over, the family sat around the dining room table and chatted until sunrise. Yes! This was a special day for the Briant boys.

David had been accepted at Syracuse University on a partial scholarship and I was accepted at Oswego State Teachers College. But when September of 1948 arrived, a decision was reached that neither one of us would be going to college: our family lacked the funds. David and I were very disappointed, but understood. We put our continuing education on hold.

Father had purchased me a stake rack Ford truck, a ton and a half and David at 16 years of age went to work at Dunn and McCarthy Shoe factory in Auburn.

I worked for Wheat Brothers, also in Auburn, hauling baled hay from the farmer's field to box cars located at different railroad sidings. The bales of hay were heavy, weighing up to 120 pounds. Loading box cars was a difficult task. The heat in the railroad cars was well into the nineties and hundreds, especially with the sun beating down on them all day.

II

Leaving Home

II

After my high school graduation I started to take night courses at the Auburn Business School: business math and accounting. However, although my grades were in the low nineties, I decided to drop out of the school, because the courses did not hold my interest.

In 1949 I entered Central Radio and Television School in Kansas City Missouri, at my father's suggestion, as he was concerned about my future career path. The school offered a six month course to become a Station Agent for one of the sixteen major airlines.

The classes consisted of typing, reservations, ticket sales, meteorology, telephone techniques, and mathematics.

There were six classes of thirty students each, from all areas of the United States.

One morning I woke up in the school dormitory with a bad toothache. I managed to struggle through the day's classes. In the evening two other students, all of us from New York State, walked to a nearby restaurant for our evening meal. I never did get to the restaurant. While en route I looked up at a large building. A sign in a sixth story window displayed the word "Dentist." I told my two friends that I was going up there and wouldn't be having supper with them. "Do you want us to go with you?" Bob said. I shook my head. "You fellas go ahead and have your dinner, I will be fine."

I made my way into the old red brick building and up a winding stairway. When I reached the sixth floor I noticed a sign on a door: "Dentist." I knocked, the door immediately swung open, and in front of me stood a bald-headed man wearing spectacles and a white frock-type jacket.

He beckoned me to come in. I can remember the cold steel blue eyes peering over the top of his glasses. I entered the office and told him my problem. "Here, sit in this chair," he said. I complied. The dentist appeared at my right side and looked at the tooth that was aching.

He immediately indicated that the tooth had to be removed. He handed me a small glass of liquid and told me to drink it. I asked him, "What is this stuff?" He replied, "This will coagulate your blood after I extract your tooth." The next thing I knew the doctor appeared with the instrument to extract the tooth. He did not use novacaine.

He reached into my mouth with this plier-type tool, and to this day I can hear the cracking of the tooth being pulled from my lower jaw. It hurt like hell! I remember that I hollered, begging the doctor, "Please stop." He just continued yanking and twisting the plier type tool. The tooth finally came out.

The doctor then gave me some cotton gauze to hold against the large hole he'd left in my mouth. I felt weak all over, and hurt more now than I had before the tooth was removed. The doctor told me, "That will be seven dollars, young man." I paid him and left his office. Every step down those rickety stairs felt like someone stabbing me in the face.

I went back to the school and when I arrived, the dormitory mother, Mrs. Conway asked me, "What happened to you?" I told this very compassionate person what had happened at the dentist's office. She asked me the name of the dentist and I couldn't remember because the pain was so overwhelming. I remember how she got me an ice pack and told me to lie down and rest.

That evening my two friends from New York took me to the City Hospital, as I was bleeding profusely. The emergency room resident doctor asked me what happened. I told him the details. The doctor packed the open hole in my mouth and sent me on my way. The two fellows who accompanied me seemed very concerned about my dilemma.

I was still bleeding heavily the following morning and the house mother contacted a dental surgeon. The dental surgeon was very kind. He indicated to me that he would have to cauterize the wound. After the surgical procedure he asked me to tell him about the dentist who had extracted the tooth. I told him all that I knew about the man. He told me that the guy who pulled my tooth must have been a "quack" and that he would contact me after his investigative inquiry.

Two days later I was interrupted in class to answer a telephone call from the dental surgeon. He informed me that the man who had extracted my tooth was posing as a dentist and asked me if I would sign a sworn statement regarding my visit to the "quack's" office. I told the dental surgeon that I would cooperate in any action against the jerk who tore my tooth out of my jaw.

I recovered and continued with my school work. The hole still remains in my jaw.

The school had an employment office for students who wished to work part-time. I applied for a job painting a garden trestle for an elderly lady who lived about ten miles from the school. I remember I had to take a street car to the location of her home. I never realized how many sides there were to a rose-garden trestle. The lady fixed me a couple of sandwiches and ice cold lemonade. She gave me eleven dollars for my efforts and seemed satisfied with the freshly painted white trestle.

For another part time job I worked in a hot-dog stand at the (then famous) Playmore Incorporated located in Kansas City. The work was mostly at night during a dancing or skating marathon. Behind the counter there was not very much room, and usually four people staffed each of the six hot-dog stands. Sometimes the pop bottles would blow up—dangerous!

On one evening about fifty women in their twenties came into the hot-dog stand area. They all wore black leather jackets, which could at first be interpreted as starlet/prostitute garb. At nineteen I was a little naive, being from a small country town in upper New York State.

I asked one of my co-workers who they were. He cautioned me not to say too much to them if they came to our stand, for they liked to pick fights with men. He then told me that they were "dykes." I asked him, "What is a dyke?" He told me that they are lesbians. I didn't ask any more questions, as I feared for my safety.

One weekend a student from Salt Lake City asked five of us if we would like to take a weekend trip to Salt Lake. On a Friday afternoon after school we all climbed into his large 1941 Cadillac Sedan and roared through the streets of Kansas City, Missouri, and into Kansas City, Kansas, and westward toward Utah. It was raining "cats and dogs."

I was sitting in the middle of the front seat. There were three in the front and three in the rear seat—with no seat belts. We had told the 21 year old driver to slow down a little, to no avail.

It was about seven miles east of Beloit, Kansas, where this huge black Cadillac we were riding in careened off the highway and went into a skid across a grassy lot. There was a crash and one of us was knocked out. I felt sharp pains as my knees struck the bottom of the dashboard. Three of the doors popped open.

When we came to our senses we learned what had happened. As the Cadillac flashed sideways across the grassy lot, it first struck a utility pole and broke it completely off. The car then swung around and struck a parked car, which, unbeknownst to us, contained an off duty hospital nurse and her boyfriend, who were in the process of doing a little "necking."

It was fortunate that the nurse was there, for she gave us all first aid. We were not happy with our 21 year old driver. Four of the occupants continued onto Salt Lake, but a fellow from Cato, New York, and I took a Greyhound bus back to Kansas City, Missouri, the next day.

The six months at Central Radio and Television School went by rapidly. Just before our last week we learned another lesson the hard way.

One evening near the end of school the three of us from New York went out on the town. It was about the only evening we had gone out. Bob, Edgar and I, in Bob's car, drove to the "Hula Hut" to watch the barely clothed dancers. I had never seen semi-strippers before.

We arrived at the "Hula Hut" at about nine o'clock. We got a table and watched a dancer do her bumps and grinds. I remember how the three of us laughed and lifted our glasses as we swilled down the beer. She came over to our table and looked each one of us in the eye with her deep set brown eyes. She didn't stop gyrating her shapely hips, and the excitement of this special attention was torture for three red blooded young American boys. She smiled at us in a flirtatious manner. We tipped her $2.00, and she continued to make her rounds to the tables of other patrons.

Bob wanted to visit another bar, and I told him and Edgar, to go ahead and that I would wait for them in the car. They left. I climbed in the back seat and dozed off.

It seemed only like a moment in time, when I was suddenly

awaken by loud hollering. Bob and Edgar had returned. In a few minutes we were in motion, with Bob driving and Edgar sitting on the passenger side of the car. I didn't realize it at the time, but Bob was having difficulty in driving. The next thing I knew we were climbing the steps of a City building. The tires were burning rubber. We had reached about the twelfth concrete step when the Pontiac coughed and died. The rubber must have smelled for blocks.

A Kansas City Police Department squad car pulled to the curb and two large burly cops approached us with their batons at the ready. I was shaking all over: this was the first time in my life that I had felt that I was really in trouble! Then I realized that I hadn't done anything wrong.

It was good ol' Bob who would have to answer their questions. I remember one of the cops saying, "What seems to be the problem, boys?" They didn't yell or act tough. I knew that we had just met two of Kansas City's finest.

They took us to the police station and told us to "set down." Bob called the dormitory mother and told her what had happened. I remember the desk Sergeant was on the telephone and talked with her.

There was more conversation with the Sergeant and the two policemen, who then came over and told us that they were not going to arrest us. But, they wanted to show us the place they call the "tank," where all intoxicated arrestees spend some time before being assigned a cell. We went with them down the hall and peeked through the smoke-stained windows covered by bars. There were drunks all over this huge room. Some were rolling around on the floor hollering and screaming. Some of them were hitting their heads on the floor as well as the wall. It was frightening to see these prisoners acting this way.

One of the policemen offered, "I don't think that you want to join these fellows in the tank, do you, boys?" "No, sir," we replied in unison. The policeman was about six-foot two and must have weighed two hundred and fifty pounds. He had an Irish face and spoke gently to us as he concluded, "Let this be a good lesson learned for you boys." We all agreed.

The police delivered us to our dormitory and told Bob that he would have to pick his car up later in the day. The dormitory mother met us at the door and told us to get some sleep. She told us sternly, "You young men were lucky. Do not let this happen again." We assured Mrs.

Conway that we would not.

At School's completion my marks indicated that I was scholastically rated in the middle of the class. I had hoped for better marks. I was disappointed. I bid farewell to all of my Central Radio and Television School friends and headed back east to New York State and my family. It had been a wonderful experience and I seemed at least intact— well, with the exception of one tooth.

The Greyhound bus trip to my native state was interesting. I wondered where all the other travelers were going. They represented every age group. Crossing the state line into New York gave me a good feeling. I had been away for six months.

The family greeted me at the bus station in Syracuse. On the way to Auburn they asked me about Kansas City and what my experiences had been. Although I had written my family regularly I wasn't able to tell them everything in a letter. I told them about school, the part-time jobs, and the accident, while en route to Salt Lake City and how the trip had ended for me in Beloit, Kansas. It was good to be home.

After I had been back a week, father drove me to Ithaca for the purpose of making an inquiry at Robinson Airline Inc. It was disappointing; there were no job openings. On the return trip home I realized that my Station Agent course that I had finished would become only an entry on my resume, because only the top third of each graduating class were being accepted for employment.

I applied for work again at the Henry & Allen Company in Auburn. My previous employment with them was noted, and I was rehired. But the grinding job, at which I had experience, was not open. So now the cutter bar inspection department had a new inspector. Because the company was a leading manufacturer in central New York, someday the cutter bars that I inspected would be attached to mowing machines for the harvesting of hay.

Missing Tuesday night drills at the armory in Auburn, especially without a legitimate reason, introduced me to the often clandestine dynamics of organizations. For the first time in my young life I would see internal politics in action. I was demoted from Staff Sergeant to Recruit. I was assigned to an SCR-300 field radio. The gentleman who replaced me in the mess hall was a very close friend of the Company Commander. My father, a veteran of World War I, was disappointed in my reduction of rank to Recruit.

The work at Henry & Allen slowed down, and being on the lower end of the seniority list, I again found myself unemployed. This occurred sometime in March of 1950.

In April of 1950 my unemployment status changed. I was hired by the Sylvania Electric Company in Seneca Falls, and assigned to the midnight shift in the Television Tube Sealing Department. For nine months I stood before a rotating unit, which required the constant lifting of the tubes onto it and removing them after they were sealed.

When I had been with the company for six months I enlisted in the United States Air Force on a delayed enlistment program. I completed an additional three months with the company giving me a total of nine months service.

It was now the middle of December 1950. Having completed my work with Sylvania Electric at this time, I said good-bye to my friends and family. My honorable discharge had arrived in the mail from Company I, 108th Infantry, 27th Infantry Division.

Father, with tear filled eyes, gave me a parting bear hug at the train station in Syracuse on December 20, 1950. I was twenty years old at this time.

The train ride to the Lackland Air Force training base in San Antonio, Texas lasted three days. I was filled with excitement and looked forward to the experience. The Korean War was beginning to expand. On my arrival at the base I encountered a great deal of activity. Hundreds of tents had been pitched to house the incoming air force recruits. Luckily I was assigned to a wooden barracks. We all assembled in front of a headquarters building.

The college boys were separated out, as were prior military-service people. With my National Guard experience I was placed in the latter group.

My basic training lasted for two weeks, after which I was assigned to a casual squadron at Westover Air Force Base in Chicopee, Massachusetts. The barrage of tests during the indoctrination indicated that my field would be in a technical area. I was slated to go to Radio and Radar School at Keesler Field, Mississippi, but there was a delay because the schools were full. The assignment to Westover was to be a stop-over until openings were available.

The train ride to Westover lasted three and one half days. My thoughts raced back to Auburn and my family and friends. I wondered what was in store for me as a member of the United States Air Force. I dozed off into a deep sleep.

The barracks at Westover were converted World War II buildings, heated with soft coal stoves. About thirty of us shared two barracks. We were assigned various duties on the base, including garbage collecting and snow shoveling.

One day as I read the bulletin board in the mess hall, I noticed an announcement: Wanted One Diet Cook, interested parties contact Captain Mary Moore, Food Service Officer. My mind was racing. Should I hold off and end up going to Keesler, or should I see Captain Moore?

Captain Mary Moore, attractive with greyish hair, and wearing air force sunglasses, told me to sit down and describe my food service experiences. When I was done telling her of my work with the National Guard, she indicated that I could start the job the next morning.

The mess hall that I was assigned served the 1600th Medical Group, and my particular assignment required me to prepare special diets for hospital patients: low salt, high fat, low fat and plenty of custard. The diets for diabetics had to be weighed and everything had to be just right. The meals were prepared and then loaded into a cart for individuals on different wards.

While I was serving the patients, the cart was plugged into electricity to keep the food hot. I enjoyed the work and met a great many people from all over the country. My past culinary experience made my diet cook position enjoyable.

One day I received a directive to prepare a special diet for an air force colonel who had just arrived at Westover from his assignment in Germany. When I delivered the diet to his room I found the door closed. I stopped the cart, applied the brake, and opened the door. I was terrified! The colonel apparently had committed suicide. The walls were covered with blood, and a shotgun lay on the floor.

I quickly notified the nurse on the ward and called the air police. The death was a horrifying experience for everyone. I learned later that the colonel, who was suffering from cancer, had smuggled the shotgun into the room. Apparently he wanted to avoid any more pain.

On my off-duty hours I had the occasion to visit various facilities on the base. The base at Westover had the usual airman's club for recreational activities. On weekends they would have dancing, sometimes with a live band, other times with the playing of records. I attended several of these dances. They were fun. The girls came from Holyoke, Fairview, Chicopee, Chicopee Falls, and Springfield.

There were other social functions available off base. On one such occasion a group of us from the base attended a church dance in downtown Springfield. A good time was had by all.

On a Saturday evening in April, 1951 I attended a dance at the Roseland Ballroom in Holyoke. I was standing with my back to a stairway. I turned around, and there was a petite young lady smiling at me. I asked her for a dance. She was Peggy Brennan from Holyoke, the daughter of a former Holyoke police officer.

Peggy and I saw each other on my days off. She was employed by the New England Telephone and Telegraph Company in Springfield. She was Irish-American and had a great sense of humor. We double dated and enjoyed talking about everything. I met her mother and father and brother. Eddie, her brother, loved to play sandlot softball, and every time I saw him in the early fifties, he was always carrying a softball glove and a bat. Peg's parents were avid Boston Red Sox fans, and the conversation over the dinner table always got around to that infamous team. We had enjoyable times.

I stayed in touch with my parents and brother and sister by mail. It was a good life for me in those days at Westover.

One day as I sat in my room at Westover just after I went off shift, I was told to contact the orderly room. The First Sergeant wanted to see me. I combed my hair and splashed some cold water onto my face.

When I entered the Sergeant's office he greeted me with a smile. "Hello, John," he said. "Did you want to see me, Sergeant?" I replied. "Yes, I wanted to inform you that you are now a Private First Class and your MOS (job description code) has been changed to 62250. You are now a senior cook and your new level includes the opportunity to advance to the rank of Staff Sergeant." He paused. "John, you also are scheduled to go overseas. You are leaving for Keflavik, Iceland in a month." "I am!" I replied. Wow! Iceland — I bet that's cold up there.

I thanked the Sergeant and left his office.

I called Peggy on the telephone and told her the news. She seemed upset. I was happy about my promotion but not quite so happy about my overseas assignment. I was looking forward to going to Korea. I realized that I had to go where they sent me. Orders were orders.

The next morning I went to see Captain Moore. She informed me that my work was excellent, but it was time to start a tour of duty overseas. The Captain advised me that I would have a fifteen-day furlough before leaving for Iceland. Although Peggy and I were not officially engaged we were becoming more than close friends. I met with Peggy and her parents and told her that I was going to take a fifteen-day leave to see my parents and family before leaving for Iceland.

August 15th, 1951 was the date that I arrived at my parents' home. Father and mother informed me that they wanted me to accompany them to the north country to say good-bye to some of our relatives. The trip to Watertown and region was enjoyable, and father seemed happy that I wasn't going to a combat zone. The fifteen days went by rapidly. I told my family that I loved them all, then left for Westover Air Force Base. I called Peggy from the base and tearfully said good-bye. We promised to write each other.

On September 1st, I found myself sitting on a canvas swivel seat in a C-54, a four engine propeller-driven transport. The plane, a military aircraft, was loaded with freight and one airman, me. This was my first plane ride. We raced down the concrete runway at Westover. I asked myself, will this plane get off the ground or will we run off the runway? As we neared the end of the runway, the plane seemed to strain. The freight straps creaked and creaked. My hands were moist with sweat. I was extremely nervous. The nose of the plane finally lifted, climbing slowly into the heavens above. We were on our way to Iceland, an island in the North Atlantic.

With sweaty hands I turned to my right and peered out at the ground below. I saw the numerous colors of the fields, the tops of houses, and other buildings. The drone of the engines was heavy and my heart felt empty, and I wondered if I would ever see this great country of ours again. One of the crew members came out of the cockpit to see if I was alright. He was a First Lieutenant.

The hours passed and we stopped over at Goosebay, Labrador. The plane continued on to Keflavik. I was soon to arrive at my new home.

It was a cloudy day and Iceland looked very bleak and desolate as I peered out the window of the plane. The freight restraints strained as the big C-54 circled the base while a Navy Fasron Patrol plane went in for a landing. My hands began to perspire. My heart pounded.

The large plane settled onto the runway and rumbled along the concrete runway. Keflavik was an International Airport and a great many civilian overseas flights stopped there. The giant plane slowed as the brakes and props eliminated the momentum. The C-54 turned and headed toward the terminal area. It came to a stop and the engines were cut off. The cockpit door opened and the air force Captain said, "Did you enjoy your flight, PFC?" "Yes, sir," I replied.

My flight bag and duffle bag were heavy as I struggled down the unloading ramp. My hands were still sweating. This is the last place I thought that anyone would want to spend a year out of their life.

I had been the only passenger besides the crew. A jeep pulled up and a Corporal told me to put my bags in the back. He said, "Welcome to the 1400th Air Base Group. The Squadron Commander would like to talk with you before I take you to your quonset hut." The land seemed very flat. There were no trees, but the smell of fish was definitely in the air. "Thank you, Corporal," I replied.

The jeep pulled up in front of a small quonset hut. A large sign hung over the entrance: "1400th Air Base Group" and, underneath, "Orderly Room." The Corporal introduced me to the Major, and I threw him a salute. He shook my hand with a firm grip and told me to sit down. He appeared to be about 45 years of age. He told me that he had been a flying officer, but problems with his eyesight forced him to ground duties. He seemed friendly and appeared very relaxed. I wasn't relaxed.

The Major told me about the mission of the U.S. Air Force in the region. He indicated that I would be in Iceland for a year, and that if I experienced any problems, either personal or job-related, that his door would always be open for assistance. I thanked the Major, saluted, and turned toward the door.

I was taken to a quonset hut by the Corporal and dropped off with my baggage. I went into the hut. A fellow was asleep in one of the beds. He was snoring. The hut was dark; the windows were covered with plastic shields. The snoring fellow coughed and sputtered and said, "Who in the hell is making all the noise?" I told him that I had just arrived from

Westover Field and was attempting to get settled. He looked up and smiled and said sarcastically, "Welcome to Iceland."

He informed me that I was to report to the mess hall in the morning. He continued to tell me a little about the base. I learned that Lockheed Air Craft Company had recently turned it over to the air force. During World War II troops en route overseas to the European Theater used Iceland as a stopping off point. I learned that Iceland experienced six months of light and six months of darkness.

Soon the night cook that I had awakened was snoring more loudly than ever. I continued to make up my bed and store my toilet articles. The shaving cream, soap, toothpaste, shaving lotion and other essentials just about fit into the small cabinet above my bed. Then, so that I wouldn't disturb the sleeping cook, I went for a walk.

It wasn't long before I found out that the base was close to a whaling station, which accounted for the strong fish odor. I wondered if I was ever going to get used to it. As I walked toward an old hangar that displayed an aging sign which read "Lockheed," I thought about Peggy and my parents and Peg's parents. I wondered what they were doing at home this very moment. I said to myself, "What the hell am I doing in this God forsaken place?" I missed Peg.

When I went to the mess hall for dinner I saw other air force members and some army personnel. I wondered what they did on the base. The mess hall was divided. Sergeant and above ate in one dining area, and the ranks below Sergeant ate in another dining area. I noticed that there were two distinct serving areas. The mess hall was old and looked like it was going to fall down.

I looked at the menu for the evening dinner and noted that oven-fried liver was scheduled along with mashed potatoes, string beans, cabbage salad, bread, butter, tea and coffee, and spiced cake topped with a white frosting. A tray of assorted pickles and relish was displayed on the serving line. The cooks looked tired, and their white uniforms were dotted with food stains. Large white hats held back their hair. They served their creations in silence. There seemed to be plenty of liver topped with onions and tomato sauce. Personally I was fond of liver and went back for a second helping.

After dinner I walked over to my quonset. I met some of the other personnel, all cooks. Some of them were from South Carolina, California,

Texas and Florida. They were playing cards.

I think sleep conquered me before my head hit the pillow. I didn't hear anything until someone's alarm went off at 3:00 a.m.. It was one of the cooks who had to be in the mess hall for early duty. I rolled over and fell into a slumber. I dreamed that the C-54 had ditched into the North Atlantic and I was trying to swim. The bed was being shaken by a fellow wearing a white uniform with a slouched white hat. He said, "Hey wake up fella you've got an appointment with Sergeant Alfonzo Unick and he wouldn't appreciate you being late." I said, "O.K. I'll go over to the mess hall as soon as I shave and shower."

The shower felt good. I had nicked my face with the razor. At 21 years of age my beard was light, but the peach fuzz still had to come off. I slid into a pair of clean fatigues and put on my shoes. I wondered what Sergeant Unick was going to be like. I'd heard he was a tough taskmaster. I made my bed and dusted around it; we had no maids in Iceland. Finally I left the hut for the mess hall.

Sergeant Alfonzo Unick was a big man of 6'2" and weighed about 200 pounds. He had a gold tooth centered right in the center of his front teeth. His jaw was firm and set. He had a mean look on his face. He was from Philadelphia.

"Well it's about time you got here," he roared! I gulped and replied, "Sergeant, I got here as fast as I could."

He went on to tell me that he was the boss and that he had been in the army air corps for 18 years, and that when the army air corps became the U.S. Air Force there was a big change. This transition was still taking place, and everyone had one or two olive drab colored uniforms, but the blue uniform of the U.S. Air Force was considered the Class A one.

I could see that Sergeant Unick was tough, but underneath that hard crust I knew that he would be a fair and reasonable boss as long as I did my job properly.

He told me that we had six air force cooks on his shift and one civil service civilian cook by the name of Alfred Brown, who was assigned just to soups and gravies. He cautioned me about the Icelandic civilians who did the K.P. (Kitchen Police) in the mess hall and dining rooms. What he meant was that none of the air force personnel should discuss anything with them with the exception of weather and other casual conversation. There was to be no conversation with them concerning air force policy.

Sergeant Unick briefed me concerning our work schedule. I would be assigned to his shift and we would work one shift on and two shifts off. The shift would begin at 10:00 a.m. and go until 7:00 p.m.. We would report the next morning at 3:30 a.m. and work until 2:00 p.m.. Then we would be off duty from 2:00 p.m. until 10:00 a.m. the day after tomorrow. He told me to report at 10:00 a.m. when his next shift would start. I thanked him and left the mess hall. Good job I thought, I just arrived and now I don't have to report for duty until day after tomorrow.

I spent the next day writing letters to Peggy and my parents. All the mail leaving Iceland went by aircraft to the States. The rest of the day, after mailing the letters, was spent cleaning my assigned area.

The quonset huts looked like a half of a 360 degree circle or one half of a cylinder lying upright on the ground. Each consisted of space for twelve people. The shower and bath were located at one end of the hut. The furnace for heating the hut was located near the shower room and also heated the hot water tank for showers and sinks. My particular hut had housed Lockheed personnel prior to the start of the Korean conflict.

The plastic shields over the windows kept the bright light out during the six-month daylight cycle. The huts were livable, but we were cramped for space.

The air force personnel were each assigned .30 caliber carbines, which were secured in locked metal cabinets. The ammunition was secured in another location.

My first duty day in the mess hall arrived quickly. Sergeant Unick was waiting to start the shift meeting. The meeting covered assignments for the preparation of the evening meal. Tonight we were having roast beef, mashed potatoes, gravy, peas and carrots, cabbage salad, cream of tomato soup, coffee, tea, milk, rolls and rice pudding with whipped cream. I was assigned to the roast beef. The other personnel were assigned the remaining menu items. When assigned to the main entree a worker was not required to help serve on one of the two serving lines.

Feeding 1200 people is not an easy task. A cook serving on the line has to deal with 1200 individual personalities. The people we serviced represented just about every state of the United States. Actually it is a training ground for practical psychologists. The cooks assigned to Sergeant Unick were all senior cooks with a 62250 AFSC (Air Force specialty classification).

Early mess was served at 4:30 P.M. this day as it was every day for air police and special line personnel. Usually about fifty people would come through our serving line at that time. At approximately 5:15 p.m. the two serving lines were open and the sound of clattering silverware and the clinking plates could be heard in each dining room area. We were ready for them. The steaming service lines bustled with activity. Today, my first day on duty at Keflavik, was an historical moment in my air force career.

The roast beef on this first day of duty apparently turned out alright, for Sergeant Unick told me that if I cooked like that for the rest of my tour I would probably be considered for a future promotion.

Many of us at Keflavik felt cheated that we didn't draw a Korean assignment. We knew in our hearts that many of our fellow Americans were suffering in Korea. We wanted to be there to offer them support. As time passed we revised our thinking and decided that everyone in the military service of our country had a mission, and ours was Keflavik assigned to the Icelandic Defense Force (IDF). I felt that the food service function of the 1400th Air Base Group was an important task and that I would do my part in making our mission a success.

I remember the day that we had a special visitor: Air Force General Curtis LeMay. His plane had stopped for refueling, and the General and two of his aides stopped by for some roast beef sandwiches. We all saluted him. He said, "At ease, gentlemen." We made some special sandwiches for these special guests. They thanked all of us and departed for Europe.

The days went by slowly, and my letter writing was important as a moral booster. The relationship with Peggy through the mail seemed to be getting stronger. She was good about writing. My parents, especially father, would send letters often. I heard from brother David and sister Joan, at least once a month.

The U.S. Air Force eliminated the olive drab uniform and we were now wearing blue uniforms. The transition from olive drab to blue began as the U.S. Army Air Corps became the United States Air Force. I can remember one day, shortly after I arrived at Keflavik. I was walking through Keflavik's International Air Port wearing my olive drab uniform. I soon felt the presence of two air policemen, one on each side of me. One of them said, "Airman you cannot wear an O.D. uniform here in the airport. Only Class A Blue uniforms can be worn." "Yes, sir," I replied. They let me off with a warning. I never donned an O.D. uniform again.

There were USAFI college courses that any member could participate in; however, I had become disenchanted because of my Oswego State Teachers College acceptance and the fact that I could not attend college in the fall of 1948. I put taking courses out of my mind. Instead I got a part-time job at the airbase Non-Commissioned Officers' Club. I could work there only on my night off-duty. It was a lot of fun and I was able to save some money, too. The kitchen at the club was small, but large enough to fry cheeseburgers, hot dogs and chicken. The fellows from the southern part of the U.S. assigned to Keflavik loved fried chicken. I told many of the club members, "Don't you fellas get enough to eat in our mess hall?" They would reply, "Cookie just because you don't drink, we do, and when we do, everybody gets hungry." All I remember is that our NCO club sold a lot of fried chicken, especially on weekends. The days were routine, and our experiences in food preparation were broadening. The food we served was based on the master menu that was sent to us from Washington, D.C.. The military personnel we served, seemed to appreciate our efforts, and naturally this response made our job a little easier. Time slipped by. I was promoted to Corporal in October of 1951. Shortly afterwards the rank was changed to Airman Second Class.

On Thanksgiving Day a special concentrated effort was put forth in our mess hall. The main entrees included not only turkey with all the trimmings, but roast of beef/au jus and baked ham as menu high lights. The base had a new bakery and they supplied pumpkin, mincemeat and apple pies. Not only did we feed our people, but several Icelandic citizens joined us for the Thanksgiving celebration. When everyone was served, all the cooks heaped our plates with baked ham and raisin sauce, then turkey with dressing.

The dressing that accompanied our big tom turkeys was special. We used three different base stocks: turkey, ham, and beef. We blended the stocks with crumbled unsalted corn bread, braised onions, celery, giblets from the turkey, dried bread, and seasonings. Then it was mixed thoroughly and placed in large pans. We beat up eggs and mixed them with a little milk and brushed the top of the dressing in the pans. We placed some bacon slices and orange slices on top and baked it at 325 degrees. It became a popular item in our mess hall, especially during Thanksgiving, Christmas and Easter.

Christmas time brought several performers from the States to entertain the military personnel. The headliner who visited Iceland was Walter Pidgeon. By this time we had just moved into a brand new mess hall. A stage had been erected. Mr. Pidgeon was very popular. There was a little excitement when Mr. Pidgeon threw a cream pie at one of his group and it missed and struck a Staff Sergeant directly in the face. The Sergeant took the mishap well, but his face became crimson. To our surprise he broke out in laughter. Walter Pidgeon apologized and everything continued in a friendly spirit. All of us stationed in Iceland appreciated the performance given. Iceland was a lonely place.

All the cooks got to know each other and we would exchange information about the cultures of our home towns and cities. I cannot remember any altercations between any of our military people.

The government of Iceland was called the "Althing." During my tour there it was difficult to learn about their culture. I did hear that a daughter of one of the government leaders attended Wells College in New York State. The Icelandic people were attractive. Blond hair and blue eyes predominated this fair-complected society. The only Icelandic people with whom I had contact were the people who worked in our dining facilities. I got along very well with them. They spoke enough English so we were able to communicate.

The Capitol of Iceland is Reykjavik, located about twenty-five miles from our base. Our U.S. Navy had a presence in the Capitol. On my only taxi ride through the capitol I noted the houses were small. The shops were clustered together. The taxi driver took me through the harbor area. He told me that a great many Russian fishing boats visited the port. He pointed out the hot springs to me and indicated that all their heating was derived from these springs. There were no trees; however, I did see some shrubbery growing in some greenhouses.

On the way back to the base the driver drove me past the whaling station. The smell of fish was ever present. From the taxi I could see the whale —massive in size being stripped of its' blubber. The taxi driver took me to the main gate of our base. He charged me 300 krona, which at the time was about $23.00. It was well worth the money to visit the Capitol even if only sitting in a taxi cab. We had been warned not to be alone. During the May Day celebration we were not allowed off the base. The two times that I was off the base were sufficient for me.

The letters kept coming and I responded to every one of them. Peggy decided that she would be my steady girl friend and told me that she would wait for me. This promise made me very happy.

The mess hall was getting to be a routine mission. The personnel were becoming quite professional in the preparation of food, and Sergeant Unick seemed pleased. He wasn't only our boss in the mess hall. He was also the person in charge of our quonset. It wasn't long before we had larger, brand new, olive drab (OD) quonset huts that housed twenty men instead of twelve. From all appearances our base was becoming larger.

Between the mess hall duties, working at the NCO club and writing letters I found very little time for anything else.

The money I received at the NCO club, both in wages and gratuities, was building up. Visions of a brand new automobile flashed before me as I diligently sent the funds to Peggy for banking. The bank interest added to the principle did not have a high yield, but my persistence in saving would insure that someday the highly polished car would become a reality instead of a dream.

It was in July 1951 when the new promotions were generated to the 1400th Food Service Squadron of the 1400th Air Base Group. The third stripe on my blue air force uniform designated that the rank of Airman lst Class had been achieved. To me, it also signified that a pay raise was forthcoming. The rank of Airman lst Class was the new classification of the old rank of Buck Sergeant.

With the promotion my responsibilities increased. I began to deal with some administrative duties. Twice a month I was assigned to the squadron's orderly room to man the telephone and pass along any important messages to my superiors. Somehow it gave me a sense of accomplishment. CQ means in "Charge of Quarters." It was during my tour of duty in Iceland that I spent some time at the Base Chapel. The chaplain was Father Brady, formerly of the Ogdensburg diocese of New York State. I took instructions and soon was baptized a Roman Catholic.

I had never been baptized into any specific religion, and attending Catholic services with Peggy gave me a sense of peace.

Although the Icelandic Defense Forces saw no actual combat, the assignment to that island country was considered a remote assignment. At 21 years of age I was blessed with strength and endurance both physically and mentally. The church did play a part in being able to withstand the lonely post that we in Iceland had been assigned to. The midnight mass performed by Father Brady on that crisp cold morning of December 25, 1951, was an event that I will always remember. The chapel was cold, and the 250 parishioners attending wore heavy parkas. We prayed to God for our families, for our service people in the Korean War, and for ourselves.

The days slipped by and the letters piled up from Peggy and my family. I made every effort to answer all of them. The writing to loved ones seem to lessen the loneliness that enveloped me.

Then came the shock during the end of August 1952, approximately two weeks from my scheduled rotation date back to the States. The letter looked normal as I hurriedly opened it, but in its pages Peggy told me of her father's passing. The way he died brought sorrow to my heart, and knowing that I couldn't be there to give her comfort and help her and Julia. The letter indicated that Peggy and her mother had returned from shopping. Nothing looked out of the ordinary until Peggy opened the bathroom door. Her father, Edward, had fallen while bathing. When he fell, his body had turned on the hot water. The final descriptive sentence told that Edward had died as a result of a heart attack. It was difficult for me to keep back the tears as I slowly replaced the letter in it's envelope.

I contacted Father Brady at the Base Chapel. He understood my sorrow. It was one of the few times in my life that people seemed to be there to help. Within thirty-six hours I had processed from the base, said good-bye to my commander and fellow associates, and found myself looking out the window of a U.S. Air Force C-97 winging our way across the Atlantic.

The orders that had been cut indicated that I was being rotated and transferred to Bolling Air Force Base, Washington 25, District of Columbia—with a thirty day furlough, before reporting for my new assignment.

The flight to the States was normal until we landed at Goosebay,

Labrador. A storm had flooded a part of the incoming runway. In the darkness when we struck the water everyone on board thought we had landed in the Ocean. Soon the C-97 was again aloft en route to Westover Field. My mind was racing. I wondered how I would find Peggy and Julia and young Edward.

It was still dark when the giant C-97 touched down on the concrete runway at Westover Field. When we deplaned, an air force bus was waiting to take us over to the customs check point. Obviously, considerable time would have to be spent going through U.S. Customs. It had been approximately two and one half hours since I had landed. The taxi I was riding in wove through the city streets, which were empty but for an occasional cat darting across the pavement. My hands began to sweat from the excitement of seeing Peggy after an absence of almost a year. The taxi pulled up in front of the Oak Street apartment building. I was here at last.

The doorbell buzzed and then the door lock clicked, allowing me entrance to the hallway.

Peggy opened the door of their apartment, and right away I saw the sorrow in her face. She looked pale, and the dark lines under her eyes were predominant.

No words were spoken between us as I dropped my flight bag to the floor. I reached out and embraced her. She sobbed. It was a happy moment for both of us. It was an unhappy moment, too. We grieved her father's passing.

I entered the apartment with Peggy, and there were Julia Brennan and Eddie. I hugged them both and assured them that it was alright to let it out and that it was alright to mourn for their husband and father.

The thirty days went by rapidly. Peggy and I took a Greyhound Bus to Syracuse. It was joyous seeing my parents, and my sis and brother. We went out to dinner with them and talked about Iceland and how the Korean War was progressing. It was a happy time being together with Peg and my family. She and I tried to keep back the sadness of her father's passing.

I proposed to Peggy and gave her an engagement ring. The diamond was small, but Peggy was pleased. Our plan was to get married in January of 1953.

During the first part of October 1952 I arrived at my new

assignment. Bolling Air Force Base was located in the southeast section of Washington, D.C., a busy place. The processing lasted a few hours. Soon I found myself in my assigned barracks, the one which housed the 1100th Food Service Squadron.

The assignment to Dining Hall #3 was beneficial to me. My barracks was close by and Dining Hall #3 was just inside the main gate. The city bus stop was just outside the main gate. Not having the benefit of a car the bus stop provided me transportation to downtown Washington.

The working assignment was the same as it had been in Iceland: one shift on duty and two shifts off duty. The dining hall consisted of two separate dining rooms with the kitchen facilities in between. It was a modern kitchen with very good equipment.

The letters to Peggy were again in motion, and through the mail we finalized our wedding plans. We set the date for January 24th, which left just a little over three months to go before the blessed event.

Working in Dining Hall #3 was a great experience. The rations were the best that the U.S. Air Force could purchase: the meat was choice, the chickens seemed fresh and the eggs were fresh. The eggs in Iceland had been either canned powdered eggs or eggs from Norway. The eggs of choice to the American G.I. is the egg from America.

Dining hall inspections were frequent. The food service officer with a rank of Captain would appear at Dining Hall #3 at least once a week. Usually the shift leader would accompany him on his rounds. Everything would be checked for cleanliness.

The dining hall was always an active place. All the assigned personnel would eventually interact with everyone passing through the serving line. It was educational and informative to all of us. Just about every State in the union was represented. Special duty people working odd shifts (air policemen, mechanics, and base bus drivers) would visit our dining hall at odd hours. Our kitchen staff would receive a telephone call alerting us to how many people we would be required to serve. Generally, this would occur during the night shift, where a cook was on duty.

The surprise visits could be from anyone, from the base commander to a congressman or other government heads. We would never know who was coming through the dining room doors. At Bolling Air

Force Base we always anticipated the President might stop in. This possibility made it imperative that our workplace was immaculate.

I well remember the Halloween of 1952. Some of our cooks went out into the countryside and visited a farm stand. They returned with pumpkins, corn stalks and different colored gourds. Everybody chipped in to decorate both of our dining rooms. Sweet cider was served on this special occasion.

On Thanksgiving Day 1952 some of our base personnel were home on a three day pass for the holiday. Those that remained enjoyed a feast for kings. The turkey with dressing, ham with raisin sauce, and roast beef/au jus along with all the trimmings, including apple, cherry, mincemeat, pumpkin pies and cake topped off this special annual holiday. All of us gave thanks.

The memory of those times and places goes beyond the thought of food and the satisfying of one's taste buds. It was the era of the Korean conflict, where young American men died in battle in the valleys and on the hills of that faraway country. Many of us had volunteered to go to Korea, but to no avail. At Bolling Field or any other military installation not connected to the battle zone, we all prayed for those brave warriors.

Christmas of 1952 at Bolling was a repeat of Thanksgiving Day. The dining halls were decorated, and the festive Christmas trees drew much attention from all of us. It was not like being home with the family, but those of us who were unable to leave the base felt it was the next best thing.

Arrangements were in place for my furlough of eighteen days. It was to begin on January 20, four days before our wedding day.

Working part-time at the Bolling Air Force NCO club had helped finance our forthcoming wedding. The four months were of excitement for me. My letters to Peggy had been frequent and both of us were looking forward to our marriage.

New Year's Eve found me working at the NCO club. One wouldn't think that a major war was taking place. The laughter and band music illustrated that America was still alive and kicking up its heels. There were eighteen waiters on duty at the club for this gala New Year's celebration. In a brief lull I found myself thinking how wonderful it would be if Peggy were with me. We both loved to dance. I soon came back to reality and took an order for eight whiskey sours. The coming of 1953 was close at hand. Two minutes to go!

The noisemakers, the horns, the laughter, the singing, the dancing, the band, the clink of glasses helped give birth to a New Year. I remember well the heavy-set girl wearing a blue dress who grabbed me and kissed me. Her heavy-scented perfume smothered me and then she was gone.

The cold morning of January 20th found me at Union Station waiting patiently for the train to arrive. My thoughts were pleasant. In four more days I would lose my bachelorhood. It never occurred to me that I might be making a mistake. My only thoughts were that this was what we both wanted: a life joined together in wedded bliss.

The train wove its way through Baltimore and eventually into New York City passing through the boroughs full of life, some people happy—and many homeless, trapped in a less fortunate state, clinging to a wine bottle as if it were a cross. Many would never know that outside of that mass of humanity were fields of clover, mountains and streams, another world besides the crowded centers for the desolate and impoverished. None would ever reside in the lavish penthouses or homes of the rich and famous. I spent most of my time looking out the windows watching the buildings, the land, the farms, and the people.

The train pulled into Springfield on time and I gathered my flight bag from the rack above my seat. I thought, "Just a few more miles and I will be there."

A taxi took me to Holyoke, about nine miles from Springfield. Holyoke was an industrial city of about 60,000 people, where Hallmark Cards are produced, the city where boxers met their match in the fighting rings. A peaceful city full of strong family roots. Predominantly Irish at that time.

Peggy answered the outside door and we embraced. At last we were together. Peggy and I spent several hours discussing our forthcoming wedding.

The next few days were busy. There was the renting of the tuxedos for the wedding party; Peggy's Irish cousins were the ushers. The flowers were ordered. Peggy and I met with the parish priest. The wedding with a high mass, was set at Sacred Heart Church in Holyoke.

January 24th, 1953 was a day of sunshine—cold, but glorious. The ceremony went well, and after the priest pronounced us man and wife, Peggy and I embraced before the whole world—well, everyone of the 150 people in the church, that is.

The wedding party moved on to the wedding breakfast, which lasted for about two hours, at one of Holyoke's finest restaurants, The Yankee Pedlar. The food was outstanding. Julia Brennan, a most lovable lady and now my mother-in-law, had not forgotten anything.

The reception took place at Peggy's home. Along with the Irish wedding, it was a special experience one could not easily forget. The food and the drinks consisted of fancy hors d'oeuvres, ham, salads, pickles, olives and more drinks. It was a gala affair.

Gifts piled high on tables revealed that we had five flat-irons, four clocks, towels, tablecloths, blankets, soaps, shaving lotions, perfumes and over seventeen hundred dollars in cash. Peggy's family members were all hard working people with hearts full of unselfish attributes. Everyone made our wedding a success.

Peggy and I left for New York City the next morning for a two-week honeymoon. She had acquired several tickets for South Pacific, a stage play, the Radio City Rockettes and several other shows. The restaurants were fabulous. The hotel where we stayed was close to all the activity. A frightening experience did occur, when we had been in New York for three days. We boarded separate subways going in opposite directions. Fortunately we found each other back at the hotel a few hours later. Both of us were in the state of panic. For the remainder of the honeymoon we clung closely to each other. It had been a frightening experience.

The honeymoon went by like a moment in time. We were impressed with New York City, the melting pot of society, the city of different cultures. We both agreed that with our having lived in areas with much less population, a move to this place would take some getting used to.

The train from New York to Springfield was loaded with daily commuters as we sped northward through southern New England. Our conversation drifted to whether or not we should buy a new car or wait till later. We agreed to wait. To my sorrow we both decided Peggy would remain with the New England Telephone and Telegraph Company. It tore me up to think that I would be returning to Bolling Air Force Base without my wife. The decision was made and we would abide by it.

With one day left of furlough, I realized that the day after tomorrow I would be returning to Bolling. I thought back in time to the older people I knew who had experienced a similar situation during World War II, when sweethearts were ripped apart by duty to country. Then reality became clear; I wasn't overseas, and Bolling wasn't that far from Holyoke. So what the hell was I worried about? In fact we were most fortunate at this time in our life.

The day for departing came. Peggy, Julia, Eddie and I enjoyed a breakfast of ham, eggs, along with cold freshly squeezed orange juice. The toast was home made bread spread with jam. The coffee's aroma filled my nostrils satisfyingly. The modest apartment contained four people sitting around an enameled kitchen table conversing about the Korean War and the many friends who were dying in the valleys and on the hills of a land we knew very little about. It was difficult to comprehend how we could be sitting here, while our loved ones were facing uncertain destinies in the heat of battle.

I took the bus to Springfield to catch the train to Washington, D.C.. The parting was difficult, but our affection for each other was strong.

Union Station in Washington was a busy place. Many service-men from all the branches made their way to the train loading areas, while others were waiting for taxis and busses. I took a bus to the base.

When I arrived at Bolling and checked in, I stopped at Dining Hall #3, where the night cook was feeding a few air policemen. I grabbed a mug, and made myself a cup of tea, and accompanied it with two slices of toast. I checked the work schedule for my next duty day, and to my surprise our shift wouldn't begin for a day and a half. I said to myself, "I'll take this time to do some laundry and pick up some articles at the base exchange."

Falling back into the routine of things doesn't take long in the military. I worked my shifts and also part-time at the NCO club. Everyone asked me, "How does it feel to be a married man?" "Great," I replied. The time seemed to slow down a little. I missed Peggy and wished that she were here.

With the lost of Peggy's father I could sense that Peggy had a great deal of concern for her mother and Eddie, too. I understood that she felt that coming to D.C. would cause her additional anguish about her loved ones in Holyoke. I understood, but it was difficult to accept.

My intention when I entered the Air Force was to spend twenty years and then retire. This plan presented a dilemma, and I knew it would have to be discussed further with Peggy.

During the next few months I worked diligently in the Food Service Squadron and continued to work part-time at the NCO Club. My telephone calls and letters to Peggy were frequent.

As I sat on my bed one day in the beginning of June 1953, a knock on my door brought me some good news. I was told that I should present myself at the orderly room of the 1100th Food Service Squadron. The airman at my door told me that I was being considered for Staff Sergeant and that I should see the First Sergeant.

When I arrived at the Orderly Room, the First Sergeant greeted me and quickly advised me that a board of review was in session for several promotions in our squadron. He told me to have a seat; the board would see me soon.

The excitement of being promoted to Staff Sergeant made my mind race. I thought, "Off-base rations, housing allowance, and privileges." Then I thought, "Am I dreaming?"

The dream became a reality. The oral examination before a board of four commissioned officers covered many aspects concerning the operation of a dining hall. Some of the questions were difficult; however, my tour of duty in Iceland, under the supervision of that tough Sergeant Alfonzo Unick had prepared me for anything. Within the week the results of the board of inquiry came out in orders from the Commander of the 1100th Air Base Group. The name John H. Briant appeared with others. I became a Staff Sergeant in the United States Air Force.

The displeasure my father had experienced when I was demoted in the 27th Infantry Division from Staff Sergeant to Private would now be vindicated.

I also thanked God for making this advancement possible. To top off my promotion, during that period of time I had some special guests from New York State. My mother and sister drove to Bolling to surprise me.

Mother and sister Joan visited the D.C. area for a few days. The three of us chatted about the happenings of Central New York. We were able to dine out at several fine restaurants.

When their visit ended, I told them to give father my love and to be sure to tell him of my promotion to Staff Sergeant. It was sad to see them leave. I had all I could do to keep the tears back. I called Peggy that night to tell her of mother's visit to Bolling with my sister. We discussed the possibility of Peggy coming to D.C. for a few weeks. Peggy informed me that she would talk with her supervisor regarding a possible leave of absence from the telephone company.

A few days passed, and in a letter from Peggy, she informed me to look for an apartment—she indicated that her leave of absence was approved, and she would arrive in D.C. in a weeks time. I was overjoyed.

I located a furnished apartment within a mile of Bolling's main gate. It was a second floor and had one bedroom.

Peggy arrived in middle of June. It was a special day for both of us. We celebrated the occasion with a bottle of champagne. Finally, we were together.

I cut my hours at the NCO Club so we could spend more time together. On my off duty days we toured D.C. and visited many of the government buildings, museums and historical places.

It was nearing the middle of August 1953. I was now the shift leader of six people. All of them were Staff Sergeants and all older than I. I was busy checking the master menu when I heard some loud cheers at the other side of the kitchen. An Airman 2nd Class had stopped by with freshly cut orders that the Korean conflict was just about over. The orders further indicated that we could receive early discharges instead of going to the end of the four year enlistment.

I called Peggy as soon as possible with the news. I had already been informed that I would be facing another overseas tour and that down the road would come my promotion to Technical Sergeant. I was twenty-three years of age and already a Staff doing work that I loved.

When I arrived at our apartment Peggy and I sat down and seriously discussed my career with the Air Force. The debate went on for a considerable time. She was opposed to me continuing my career in the service. I knew at this time if my marriage was to survive I would have to give up my Air Force career. I reluctantly decided to take the early discharge offer.

On August 31, 1953 I was honorably discharged, assured of three hundred dollars mustering out pay and we returned to the Oak Street apartment and Julia and Eddie.

III

A New Career:
A New York State Trooper

III

September was a busy time for Peggy and me. We purchased a brand new green 1953 Plymouth Cambridge. The funds we used to make the purchase were from the monies I had sent to Peggy during my tour in Iceland. We paid cash; there were no car payments. The car drove beautifully. It was sharp with glistening white side walls and waxed exterior.

I applied for employment at the Springfield Armory, a large munitions plant. The position was that of a machine drill press operator. It was my job to bore holes in 50 Caliber machine gun barrels, a job that required I stand during my entire shift, except for lunch and two ten-minute breaks. It soon became monotonous. The day shift that I was assigned to began at 6:00 AM and concluded at 2:30 PM. The job did have good benefits, including hospitalization and a retirement plan. Counting my military time with the 27th Infantry Division and the U.S. Air Force, I had a total of five years and eight months toward my seniority for the retirement plan.

When I got out of work in the afternoon I would drive to the Friendly Ice Cream Store, have a sandwich, and wait for Peggy to get out of work at 4:45. Then we would ride home together in the late afternoon. Peggy rode to work with a co-worker from the New England Telephone Company. Julia and Eddie would be waiting for us when we got home. We would usually dine together. Julia would serve franks and beans on Thursday—a New England delight. The beans tasted delicious with cider vinegar, accompanied by the franks set deep into fresh hot dog rolls covered with pickle relish and mustard.

Another custom for Irish Catholics, on Friday evenings, were the fish and chips. The fish store was just a block away from our Oak Street address. The breaded fried fish and the chips were crispy and hot.

During the latter part of September I took the New York State Police examination, held at several locations throughout New York State. The site that I selected was the Armory located in Syracuse.

Peggy didn't object to me taking the examination for Trooper, but informed me that she was not going to move out of Massachusetts. I didn't take her seriously about not leaving the State, and figured she would do so if I successfully passed the examination.

During this period I took another examination, for the position of lineman with the New England Telephone and Telegraph Company. Peggy seemed pleased about the possibility that I would succeed in becoming employed with this company.

I still did not give any credence to the fact that if I were successful in obtaining employment with the Troopers, she wouldn't accompany me to New York State. In my own mind I was convinced that even though the Springfield Armory job was secure it did not appear to have any promotional advantages. I had it in my mind that I wanted to better myself.

It had been very difficult for me to give up my Air Force career, especially after I had achieved the rank of Staff Sergeant and the assurances from my superiors that there would be more promotions in my career field. The transition from the supervisory position I held in the military to a drill press operator certainly didn't appear to me as bettering myself.

In late October of 1953 my anticipation ceased when on the same day I received two letters. One was from Springfield—the New England Telephone and Telegraph Company— and the other was from Albany— the New York State Troopers. I had successfully passed each of the examinations. I was accepted as a lineman-trainee, and I had passed Part A of the State Troopers Examination and was now directed to appear at the Headquarters of the New York State Troopers on a specific date if I were interested.

My reply to the telephone company was in the form of a telephone call to their employment office. I thanked the personnel manager for his considerations and turned the job down.

I opted to continue my interest in obtaining employment with the New York State Troopers. I drove to Albany and reported to the Headquarters of the New York State Troopers. After a physical examination and oral interviews with command personnel, I was told that a background investigation would be conducted on me in New York State, Massachusetts, the District of Columbia, and Keflavik, Iceland.

On my return trip to Holyoke I thought about what it would be like to become a Trooper. Having been in the military, I was convinced that I could handle the challenge of becoming a police officer.

When I arrived at the apartment, Peggy was waiting for me. She seemed quiet and asked how I had made out with my interview and physical. I told her that I would be notified in a couple of weeks concerning the outcome of my visit to Albany. I mentioned to Peggy that there would be a background investigation conducted.

About two weeks went by and one day while I was working at my drill press the foreman came over to me and said, "There is a tall gentleman in my office that would like to talk with you. He told me that he was Sergeant Smith of the New York State Troopers."

I went immediately to the office. The well dressed gentleman in civilian clothes introduced himself to me. He showed me his identification.

He told me that he had driven down from Albany and would be in the area for a few days to investigate my background. He also informed me that another member of the New York State Troopers would be conducting a similar investigation in my neighborhood in the Auburn area of New York State. We conversed for about an hour. He was very polite, After the conversation was completed he assured me that I would be hearing from the State Troopers in the very near future.

Some of his conversation dealt with what Peggy thought of her husband becoming a State Trooper. Also what type of car I owned. He told me about some of the duties of the Trooper and the prestige that the New York State Troopers enjoy as an elite police organization.

My foreman approached me after Sergeant Smith had left. The foreman wished me good luck and told me that the Springfield Armory appreciated my work. He told me that there would be little chance for promotion working for the Armory. The foreman seemed very happy for me. He told me in parting, "He was a big fellow. I bet no one fools with that guy."

When Peggy got into the car in front of the Telephone Company, after work, she told me that she had met Sergeant Smith that morning. There was very little conversation on the way home. I advised her that if I were accepted into the Troopers I would be leaving for New York State.

I could feel some tension building between Peggy and me. I had given up my Air Force career, and now my wife didn't seem pleased with the new career that I had selected. It was the matter of making a living. Jobs were scarce, and I was looking for a secure job that I would enjoy. The situation presented a dilemma. I was apprehensive.

At the end of November 1953 a letter arrived from Division Headquarters of the New York State Troopers, directing me to report to Troop D Headquarters, Oneida, on December 16th. I had been accepted for employment. Peggy told me that she would not move to New York State. I called my father and told him the news of my acceptance. Father seemed pleased.

I contacted the Springfield Armory and the Personnel Director congratulated me on my new employment. He indicated that he would forward my final paycheck to me. He also advised me that it would not be necessary for me to give a two-week notice that I was leaving the company. My vacation credits would apply to that period of time.

Julia and Eddie, when told of my new job acceptance, wished me the best of luck. I told them that Peggy was not coming to New York State with me at this time. Julia felt that Peggy should be with her husband on this move. But it was finally concluded that Peggy would remain with her mother and brother and continue her employment with the Telephone Company. I was devastated by her decision.

On December 16 I departed from Holyoke with sadness in my heart. It was 6:00 A.M. when I pulled from my parking space in front of the Oak Street apartment building. I remember well driving through the Berkshire Mountains. There was snow on the ground. Once in a while the rear end of the little Plymouth would slide to the highway's edge as it climbed the mountain road.

About six hours later I pulled into the Troop "D" Headquarters parking area located on Route 5, a short distance from the City of Oneida. On that cold day the American flag was flying and furling from the large flagpole situated in front of this most impressive building.

The first person I met was First Sergeant William Keeley. He welcomed me to Troop "D" and indicated that he had been expecting me. Sergeant Keeley was in uniform and presented himself in a military manner. I remember him as a person with dignity, a true gentleman. When he spoke to a person he looked that person square in the eye. He was a man of authority. That afternoon he escorted me through the Headquarters and made me feel comfortable.

Each Troop Headquarters in those days had a dining room, in which the personnel would partake of their meals. I remember my first meal at Troop "D"; roast chicken with mashed potatoes, gravy, vegetable, green salad and dessert. Coffee, tea and milk were available. It was a custom that the troopers spoke very little during the meal. This "rule" applied especially to the rookie Trooper.

Another rookie arrived on December 16th. Robert Orr was a quiet fellow. He seemed very intelligent. We spent the first week in indoctrination: interviews with the Principal Clerk, Sergeant E.E. Stickels, who swore us in. Each of us raised our right hands and repeated the oath. After the swearing in ceremony, Sergeant Stickels assured us that we were now Troopers. Rookies, but still Troopers.

Supply Sergeant Eugene Arnold, issued uniforms to both of us: several shirts, breeches, ties (purple in color), tie bar, two Stetsons, two collar ornaments, several pair of grey socks, a pair of leather puttees, spurs, dress blouses, overcoat, rain coat, a .45 Caliber Revolver and ammunition, overshoes, foot rubbers, flashlight with batteries, bulletin binder for memos, and a nightstick, along with handcuffs and key and Summons Holder.

Sergeant Arnold was a very disciplined Trooper. He was strict, but seemed to be a fair man. He told us to make certain that we took very good care of our assigned equipment. There were other small items assigned to us, such as plenty of black shoe polish and extra shoe-strings. The only thing we had to buy was our underwear.

Two other important items were issued to us. One was the State Trooper Badge. It was silver, and my assigned number was Shield D-133. The second item was the Identification Card bearing the name of the Trooper with a photograph attached. It was signed by the Superintendent of the State Police, Albin Johnson.

The New York State Troopers was a semi-military organization, and in the initial creation of this rural police organization it was mounted. The Troopers patrolled the rural areas of the State on horseback. The early members of the organization brought much needed law and order to communities they patrolled.

Bob Orr and I, both rookies, at Troop "D" spent several hours a day doing some dry firing with our assigned .45 Caliber Revolvers. We received instruction to acquaint us with the basics of our new profession.

I had been a member for about two weeks when I realized that it was becoming most difficult for me to be away from my wife. I knew the reason that she didn't want to make the move to New York State was her concern for her mother. I respected Peggy for her stand on this issue, and was torn inside. At the end of the two-week period I made out my resignation and gave it to the First Sergeant. He told me that I shouldn't be hasty about my decision. He advised me that he would give me a few days to go back to Massachusetts and talk it over with my wife.

The return to Massachusetts only made matters more complicated. Peggy was steadfast in her decision to stay with her mother and Eddie. Julia was torn too. She tried to get Peggy to change her mind.

I called my father, and he informed me that it was the wife's place to join her husband wherever the husband was employed. Father told me that it was my decision to make. He did not want to interfere.

After three days I returned to Troop "D" and asked the Sergeant if it were possible to withdraw my resignation. He indicated that it would be necessary to take the matter up with the Troop Commander. First Sergeant Keeley called the Troop Commander, who was attending a funeral in another part of the State. The Troop Commander consented to the withdrawal. I was immediately reinstated.

I prayed to God to give me strength to withstand the sadness that I experienced in my wife's refusal to join me in New York State. My prayers were answered.

My first assignment was the Pulaski Barracks of the State Troopers. This assignment was effective the first part of January 1954.

Before reporting to Pulaski I drove to the Auburn area to stay overnight with Mother and Father. They greeted me with open arms. We talked and talked. Father took a couple of pictures of me and wanted to try on my Stetson. He tried on the overcoat, too. Both of my parents felt badly about Peggy not moving to New York State. This situation was difficult for all of us.

They were all waving at me when I pulled out of the driveway of my parents' home. Here I was in uniform, headed to my first official assignment, Pulaski, New York. I made my way back to Syracuse and then north on Route 11. It was snowy and cold.

On the way to Pulaski I stopped at several stores and purchased a comb and some candy bars. I arrived at the Pulaski Barracks at about 11:00 o'clock in the morning.

I entered the front door of the Station. The first thing I saw was a buffing machine being operated by a large burly trooper with a gruff look on his face.

The Trooper looked up and immediately shut off the buffing machine. He spoke first, "My name is Al Secor. I am going to be your Senior Trooper. Welcome to Pulaski."

"Yes sir. I am glad to be here."

Trooper Secor was a big man with a receding hairline. He told me that he had been a member of the State Troopers for five years. He went on to tell me that the work week was about 120 hours. (My starting salary was about $3,000 per year plus $4.25 per day for meals when I was not assigned to Troop Headquarters.) He told me that I would be riding with him on patrol for about two months, and that I should refrain from unnecessary conversation but, if I had an intelligent question, he would attempt to answer it. I could sense that Trooper Secor was in charge, and I quickly resigned myself to the fact that I was definitely the "Rookie."

I was assigned a bedroom, with a bed and a mirrored dresser, and a closet for my uniforms. All members entering the State Troopers during the time of my enlistment were each also assigned a foot locker. Mine would be stored in the attic area of the barracks.

The sheets and pillowcases were changed each week by each Trooper, who was responsible for maintaining his bedroom area. All beds were made each day. The rooms were always kept neat and ready for inspection at any time of the day or night.

During the period of time prior to 1960 the barracks of the Troopers were their home away from home. Time off consisted of two nights a week and one four-day pass a month. The night off time changed over the years. I remember going off duty at 5:30 one evening and reporting for duty at 10:00 the next morning. The change took place when I went off duty at 3:00 in the afternoon and reported for duty at 12:00 noon the next day. The free period did not afford time enough to go very far. I can remember spending many nights, while on pass, reading my manuals in my bedroom. It became apparent that the Trooper's life was difficult, especially if he were married.

      I was under the close direction of Trooper Secor for about two months. I accompanied him on all assignments and uniform investigations. The State Troopers consisted of the uniform force and the BCI (Bureau of Criminal Investigation). The uniform Troopers were usually the first on the scene, and the BCI would assist the uniform Troopers on complex cases. An example could be a burning of a building where the cause was suspicious. The uniform Trooper would conduct a preliminary investigation. During the investigation, if evidence emerges that would tend to show that the fire had been deliberately set, the Bureau of Criminal Investigation would adopt a case on the suspicious fire and continue a thorough investigation. If a suspect were identified and there were sufficient proof showing that the person actually set the fire, that person would be arrested for a degree of arson. The rules and regulations clearly designate which cases will be investigated by members of the BCI. Trooper Secor was strict and fair. A patient man, he explained the workings of the State Troopers with the wisdom of a college professor. I learned that it was to my advantage to listen to him with my undivided attention. In the early days, with a small salary, there were not the extra dollars to buy a steak for my evening meal. Many evenings and during lunchtime Al would take me to his home, where his lovely wife would exhibit her talents in the culinary arts. It became very apparent to me that the troopers were a special breed of men. They took care of each other and it became more evident as my career continued.

      I studied the Trooper manual with intense excitement. The theme that impressed me without hesitation was the ideology of helping your fellow citizen. The Troopers performed a very delicate and important function for the people of the State of New York. They were unique. At the time of my enlistment I believe that the six troops that covered New York State had about 850 to 900 members. They all lived in a barracks environment. Each Trooper knew his assigned district very well.

My tutorial period with Trooper Secor came to a close. I had learned a great deal working with him. The accident investigations, the family/domestic complaints, people arrested for Public Intoxication, the simple assault cases and even the traffic violations all added to my Trooper experience. It was a time of molding myself into a workable, independent thinking Trooper. A Trooper who could make the proper judgement calls on rather difficult encounters. This learning process, which needed my close attention, was important.

The discipline instilled in each Trooper was an important ingredient of the training phase. In those days when a Senior Trooper gave you an order or command, a rookie didn't hesitate, but performed the required task.

There were other Troopers—senior to me—assigned to the Pulaski barracks. I can remember the first week that I was allowed to patrol alone. One particular day I would rather forget, but I have to share it here anyway.

On a Sunday I was on patrol in the southern district of the Pulaski's area of responsibility. Here I was, a new rookie on the job, behind the wheel of a 1952 Ford patrol car, eagerly looking for violations. On the front seat was my summons holder filled with thirteen of the Troop "D" Traffic Summons from the block of twenty-five I had been issued. Are you still with me, reader? I thought that what I was doing was one of my sworn obligations as a member.

On this particular day I found those violations. Speeding, passing a stop sign, failure to keep right, crossing a double line, passing a red light. All good violations with a ticket issued for each one.

As I said, it was on a Sunday. I was in Central Square, New York. I observed a car with a very loud muffler coming around a corner. The car pulled into a church parking area. The two people who got out of the car were quite elderly. I saw them both enter the church. My thoughts were to wait near the church, however I continued my patrol.

I didn't have a special plan to stake out the parked car with the loud muffler. I did come by the church as the services ended. I saw the elderly couple enter their car and proceed out of the churchyard. I followed them. The noise that the muffling system made was exceptionally annoying, loud and harsh, and was in fact a violation of the New York State Vehicle and Traffic Law.

The 1952 Ford troop car performed well as I pulled the elderly couple to the side of the road near the church. The man was driving. I politely asked him for his New York State Driver's License and Registration. He complied without hesitation. I told the gentleman that he was in violation of the law. I informed him that a traffic summons was being issued for an inadequate muffler. He told me that he understood.

I went back to my troop car and proceeded to write the violation. I had just started writing when I heard a woman's voice.

"How dare you stop two old people who just got out of church. What do you think you are doing?"

I politely responded, "Kindly go back to your vehicle Ma'am."

She did not comply with my reasonable request. Instead she started hollering and calling me disgusting names that would be considered obscenity if they were printed.

I kept right on writing.

I went back to the car and handed the gentleman his summons, telling him when to appear at the local Justice of the Peace. The gentleman thanked me, however his wife continued to scream and curse. I told the man's wife that I was just doing my job.

I returned to my troop car and drove away. I looked in my rearview mirror and saw the lady standing in the road shaking her fist at me.

The book on my front seat contained no more usable summons. I had issued thirteen of them in about a four-hour period of time.

When I radioed the Pulaski barracks I asked the desk man to have the remaining 12 unused summons I had left in my room at the barracks relayed to me in the Central Square area. There was a long pause before the desk man replied.

"Trooper, return to the station immediately".

When I arrived at Pulaski I soon found out that in my eagerness to perform my duty on that Sunday, I had been a little overzealous. As my reward, I was given the silent treatment for a week by my associates.

During that week I thought several times about my interview with the Superintendent of the State Police at Albany. I went back in my mind to the waiting room where I sat before seeing the Superintendent. I remembered the uniformed trooper who politely informed me, "The Superintendent will see you now, Mr. Briant. Just knock on that door."

John Briant and his Dad in the North Country, 1930.

John, Sunday April 5, 1931.

John Briant, Watertown, 1933.

David and John Briant, Amboy, NY 1937

A family gathering in 1936. Back row, left to right, Carl Walts, Henry Briant, Grandfather, John D. Briant, Dad, Elmer Appenceller, George Timmerman , Grandfather. Middle row: Sara Walts, Marjorie Briant, Mother, Bernice Timmerman. Front row: Ione Timmerman, John and his GrandmotherJessie Timmerman.

David and John Briant, 1948.

John Briant and Ray Bennett, attending school in Kansas City, 1949.

PFC John Briant with his Mother, Sister Joan and his Dad, 1951 North Country.

John in Keflavik, Iceland, 1952.

1st Sgt. Tom Tomackeski and John, USAF, 1951.

John H. Briant stands outside SP Pulaski, Troop D, 1954.

TPR John Briant on the job in Waterloo, NY at the scene of an accident involving a train and a truck loaded with apples, 1954. Note the spurs.

I remembered knocking on the door and hearing the voice from within say, "Come in."

As I opened the door my eyes saw the back of a large black leather swivel chair. It slowly turned to the right for one hundred and eighty degrees, and there sat a large man in his late forties. His hair was groomed immaculately. He was wearing a dark blue suit.

The man spoke first, "Come in, Mr. Briant, and tell me why you want to be a New York State Trooper."

I sat directly across the desk from New York State Police Superintendent Albin Johnson.

He looked directly into my eyes and said. "Well, begin, Mr. Briant."

I had a difficult time finding the words to respond to Superintendent Johnson's question. It was just like the time I had to present myself before Arthur A. Gates, my high school principal, and explain why I punched the bully in the face when the bully picked on a small child on the school bus.

I told the Superintendent that I wanted to serve the citizens of New York State to the best of my ability. I told him that I wanted a challenge and a secure career. I also told him that as a young man driving a Model "A" Ford I was stopped by a Trooper for a routine check and what a gentleman that Trooper had been to a seventeen-year-old. I told the Superintendent that from that day on all I could think about was being a Trooper.

The Superintendent went on to tell me that Sergeant Smith's investigation into my background reflected that my wife was not in favor of my employment with the State Troopers. I remembered telling the Superintendent that if I were qualified for the position of Trooper, that was what I wanted to be.

It was the parting words of Superintendent Johnson that I'll always remember. "Mr. Briant, always remember that a tough Trooper doesn't necessarily mean how strong a man is physically. It is the common sense that he applies while carrying out his duties."

It was the full week of silence from my fellow troopers that jolted my thinking processes. Apparently I got carried away and did not rely on good common sense on that day in Central Square near the church with the request I had made over the radio for additional summons.

A good lesson was learned.

An example of helping people was the night that a red glow was observed in the sky near Parish, New York, when Trooper George Loomis and I were on night patrol. We soon found the fire scene, which was a large dairy barn just on the outskirts of the town. George told me to run down to the fire station and break the alarm seal, while he went to the farmhouse to awake everyone.

The Parish volunteer fire department's siren was loud and eerie on this cold brisk morning.

Trooper Loomis proceeded to the rear of the large white farmhouse. He found an elderly man standing on the rear porch looking terrified at the burning cow barn. Trooper Loomis at this time hollered to the sleeping family in the farm house. I ran from the fire station toward the farm after setting off the alarm. The volunteer firemen responded within minutes. When I arrived at the farmhouse I saw several family members leave it dressed in their night clothing.

George was in the process of interviewing the elderly man when I arrived. From the interview we learned that the grandfather had gotten up early to start the morning chores. In doing so he lit a kerosene lantern, which fell over into some hay and ignited an uncontrollable fire. Many of the cattle, as well as the young stock, died in the blaze. If we had been a few minutes later in arriving, possibly some of the farm family could have been injured or died. It was tragic about the herd of cattle, but at least there was no human life lost.

May of 1954 arrived. Time had come for me to attend the New York State Police School held in Troy.

Once again I loaded my 1953 Plymouth with the foot locker filled with the necessary clothing for my trip. The housing was to be furnished by the State at the Hendrick Hudson Hotel in the City of Troy. It took me about three hours to drive from Pulaski to the hotel. When I arrived, I observed other rookie Troopers unloading their cars. They carried their clothes and foot lockers into the hotel. A list of room numbers and personnel assigned to the rooms was located on a bulletin board in the lobby.

This was the start of the 45th session of the New York State School for Police, authorized by the Board of Regents of the University of the State of New York. It was our official schooling to learn the processes that help make a Trooper. The session period was for May and June of 1954, and the class consisted of forty-three members of the New York State Troopers. The students were from all parts of the State.

The Director of the School was Francis McGarvey. During the two months that followed, the pressure was intense. We covered the historical significance of the State Troopers from their origin to the present date. We studied the numerous laws, including the Penal Law, The Consolidated Laws, The Conservation Laws, The Code of Criminal Procedure, The Vehicle and Traffic Laws and The Agriculture and Market regulations.

Our instructors covered in-depth the Rules and Regulations of the New York State Police. The function of the police organization depended heavily on the rules and regulations. It was the bible of the Troopers.

Many long hours were spent in the classrooms, and during the evening we forty-three rookies were busy typing the day's work. The hours of typing formed the contents of individual notebooks that prepared us for our complex examinations on police theory held each Friday afternoon.

During the session at Troy there was little time for personal business. At the end of each day's session we forty-three rookies would generally dine at various restaurants in the area. In the evenings (after typing our daily notes) we would gather in groups and test each other on various aspects of our newly chosen profession.

Every phase of our schooling was a learning experience. In addition to the classroom theory and intense indoctrination, we visited a range to fire our issued .45 Caliber revolvers and our .30 .30 Caliber carbine rifles. We became proficient in the handling of these weapons, along with the art of using a nightstick, sometimes referred to as the baton. During some of the evening sessions we studied first aid and were issued first aid qualification identification cards. We practiced on one another, tying bandages, acquainting ourselves with the various splints, becoming adept in techniques of carrying and caring for injured parties. All the instruction and the classroom experience was welcomed by us rookies.

The mid-wife course for delivering a new baby was unique. We learned how to cut the cord and how to care for the infant, as well as the mother, at birth. Little did we really believe at the time that many of us would be called upon in the normal course of our duties to deliver a child when the stork couldn't make it to the hospital.

The driving of a police car, aka troop car, is a responsibility that weighs heavily on the mind of every officer. We covered the techniques of emergency driving, and pursuit driving. How to pull a car over for a routine check or force to a stop a fleeing felon bent on freedom.

The four or five months of patrol work with a Senior Trooper prior to the academy training was very beneficial. It gives the rookie trooper a sense of his duties and the seriousness that goes along with the position of Trooper. I want to make it very clear that the New York State Troopers is an organization that had full police power in the State of New York.

To the best of my memory no one dropped out of the 45th session while in attendance. Everyone gave a concentrated effort to learn the theory and the subject matter of each course included in the session. It was one of the most memorable times in my life. During the course of my career I attempted to keep track of members attending the 45th session. In my mind they were some of the finest in the Troopers. The academy of that era, and the teachers and instructors representing it, instilled the ideology of individualism in each member.

June 19, 1954 was our graduation day. Troopers of the 45th session graduated from the New York State School for Police at Troy, New York. Each graduate had a sense of accomplishment. My memory raced back to the Syracuse Armory where it had all begun. The State wide examination of 5,000 applicants had produced only 125 acceptable candidates and out of the 125 only 50 people were hired in 1953. It gave each of us graduating a special personal pride to know that out of the 50 applicants chosen, only 43 of us graduated from the academy.

All the notable high-command people attended the graduation. Each of us received a firm handshake and a hearty "congratulations" from the Superintendent, accompanied by the diploma signifying our success. Photographs were taken of us in a group. It was a glory day for all of us.

I was very happy and proud, but deep within myself was a tearing conflict concerning my marriage and the absence of Peggy at my graduation. Had we been too hasty to join together in wedded bliss? Had we been too immature to accept the challenge of marriage? There seemed to be love on each of our parts. Should I have returned to Holyoke and worked for the New England Telephone Company or returned to the Springfield Armory? These doubts churned my guts and tore me apart inside.

I was now twenty-four years old, and even though my heart was breaking I had made a definite decision to continue my career as a New York State Trooper.

The 1953 Plymouth was again loaded with my foot locker and now the memories of the 45th session. I didn't have to report back to the Pulaski barracks for a couple of days, so I headed to Auburn to visit my parents. Thinking ahead, I had called my mother to alert her that I would be spending a couple of days at the family home.

When I pulled the Plymouth into the driveway late on June 19, all the lights were on. Father answered the door. Sister Joan rushed past him and planted a big kiss on the end of my nose. Everyone congratulated me on my graduation. Mother hugged me, too, and asked me if I were hungry.

The hotcakes that only mother could make comforted my empty stomach. The coffee was steaming hot. The crisp bacon taunted my sense of smell. Questions came from all directions about Peggy, the Police School and what it felt like to be a State Trooper. We talked into the early morning hours before sleep overpowered us.

As I drifted into sleep, my thoughts returned to my childhood. I couldn't help but think about the strappings my mother had executed on my backside as a child. A child who loved his mother so very much. Had she forgotten about that as she placed the tender hotcakes on my plate.

The time passed by rapidly, and early in the morning of my departure I thanked father, mother and sister for the wonderful two days. As I pulled out of the driveway I returned their waves with the beep of the horn. Dressed in my heavy gray uniform, I was headed to Pulaski and police work.

The Troopers' barrack at Pulaski was still there, standing adjacent to Route 11. The American flag was furling in the breeze. I was glad to be back. I wondered if my fellow troopers would share in my feelings.

The minute I entered the barracks, Al Secor came up to me and extended his hand in greeting. He told me, "I heard you did well at Troy. Congratulations." The rugged image that Al Secor projected was somewhat superficial, for under that hard crust was a compassionate man with an intense concern for society. Al Secor had shared his knowledge and wisdom with me during those early days. I will never forget Al or his lovely wife, Grace, who opened their home and hearts for a hurting young rookie Trooper in early 1954.

Al Secor was transferred to the Camden barracks just before I was transferred to Ovid. The day Al left I thanked him for his instruction, and we chatted about the few months that we had shared together. We talked about all the log trucks that he had ordered me to climb so I could hold one end of the measuring tape. We relived in memory the night we were called to a tavern fight at Panther Lake and the arrest of an intoxicated man who wanted to take on the world. The serious accidents that we investigated together. The many posted properties that we checked periodically. And, of course, the lunches and the dinners at his home.

While I was under the direction of Trooper Secor I had been introduced to all the officials of every town in our patrol district: the supervisors, road superintendents, justices of the peace, school officials, and the many unsung heroes of every community from Brewerton to Sandy Creek. It was these people and the entire community who were so important to the Trooper in his everyday performance. Especially essential are the postmasters and all the other law enforcement agencies. In every assigned area across the State of New York the Trooper depends on the expertise of these considerate people. In turn, the Trooper assists many of these people when called upon and within the Rules and Regulations of the Division of State Police. It was, and always will be, a two-way street: one helping the other through a most complex society.

I would be remiss if I didn't mention the equally important volunteer fire departments, the rescue equipment, the crossing guards, the nurses, the doctors, the clergy and those lovely waitresses who strive to please everyone. I experienced the sense of complete cooperation with everyone. A Trooper with any vision at all is aware that on any given occasion, past or present or future, it could be any one person who may help him conclude a complex case or even save his life. It should always be remembered that being a policeman is not just carrying a gun or a badge. There are many more aspects to consider.

The Village of Ovid, New York, is situated in the Finger Lakes

Region, in the southern sector of Seneca County, between Cayuga Lake and Seneca Lake.

The transfer to Ovid had not come as a surprise to me, for we had been instructed that during the first two years in service a Trooper should expect several transfers. This policy did not necessarily apply to everyone. In my case, it did, so I accepted it.

The trip from Pulaski to Ovid was quite scenic, especially in the Finger Lakes Region. It was in the summer of 1954, and vacationers were camping near and at the lakes. The Air Force training base at Sampson was still in operation, but soon to close. It brought back memories when I drove by it. I remembered when my father had worked at Sampson during World War II, when it was called the Sampson Navy Training Station. I had visited the base then when I was thirteen. Now, eleven years later, I found myself being assigned to the area as a Trooper.

The Ovid State Police barracks was a small three bedroom ranch. I would be the rookie Trooper of three assigned to that barracks. When I got out of my car, I went to the front door and was greeted by the smiling face of John Spanbauer, the Trooper in charge. The other Trooper assigned there was Glen Prosser. Both indicated they were glad to see me coming aboard. John showed me through the station and assigned me a bedroom.

It took a while before I had everything in place. The footlocker was stored in the attic. The closet was filled with my uniforms, extra stetson, shoes, rubbers and overshoes. My toilet articles were placed in the top drawer of the dresser, and underwear and other clothes distributed through each of the other drawers. I placed a picture of Peggy on the dresser. I was now at my new home.

Trooper Spanbauer had been a member of the U.S. Navy. He seemed like a friendly chap. Glen Prosser was a little more reserved.

The same schedule applied in Ovid as in all the rest of the State Police barracks throughout New York. The work week was about one hundred and twenty hours, with two nights a week off and a four-day pass each month. The pay raises came in increments, and at that time I wouldn't be at top pay as a Trooper for at least seven years. I had a long way to go.

I rode patrol with Trooper Spanbauer for about a week before I rode alone. He introduced me to all the notables. The area was a mixture of residences and dairy farms. The Seneca Ordinance Depot, Sampson Air Force training station, and the Willard State Hospital were the largest institutions in our patrol district. There were several restaurants and gas stations. There was a VFW in the Ovid area, as well as other clubs. It appeared to be a rather peaceful community. Routes 96, 96 A and 414 were our main highways, all two-laned, and curvy in many locations. I liked the area.

Thoughts of my wife were with me each night when I went to bed. It haunted me that she was so steadfast in her feelings about staying in Massachusetts. I tried not to think about it, but worry crept into my inner thoughts and gnawed at my guts. I made a special effort not to let my anxiety interfere with my performance as a Trooper.

One particular night I was on patrol and parked near the four corners just outside of Ovid, in order to watch traffic and keep an eye on two business locations nearby, one of them a gas station. Usually we went into the barracks around 11:00 p.m., but I was working alone and stayed out a little longer. It was quite a black night. I looked at my watch with my flashlight and saw that it was 1:00 a.m..

All of a sudden a car pulled in between the gas pumps of the gas station and the driver shut his lights out. The car looked like a convertible from where I was sitting. I couldn't see very well what was going on. I waited a couple of minutes, then pulled my troop car toward the gas station without my lights on. I pulled in perpendicular to the parked car and put on my high beams. The operator of the car was at the door of the gas station and appeared to be about ready to break in. My lights startled him, and he ran to the car, which I could now see was probably a Chevrolet convertible. He got into the car and sped onto Route 96A with me in hot pursuit.

We reached the speed of 85 miles per hour. I called the Troop "D" Headquarters over my radio and asked them to contact a Trumansburg patrol car. Headquarters responded that there were no patrols available to assist me with the speeding car. I was approaching the rear of the car when it turned off Rt. 96A onto a dirt road. I followed, but it was difficult to see. I rolled my driver's side window down, removed my .45 caliber revolver from the holster, and fired a warning shot, hoping that the operator of the fleeing car would pull over. The air became so dusty that I could no longer pursue the vehicle. He could have gone anyplace. I still was not familiar enough with the district to know every nook and cranny. Disappointed, I returned to the barracks and went to bed.

The telephone rang, awakening me at about 7:30 a.m.. I answered and a voice said, "The car you were chasing last night is parked on a side street in Interlaken with no plates on it. If you want to come down I'll try to help you." The caller identified himself as an Interlaken resident and told me that he had heard about the car over his police monitor. I told him that I would meet him at the place where the car was abandoned.

I got dressed and signed out of the barracks, indicating that I was going on GHP (general highway patrol) to Interlaken, relative to an abandoned vehicle.

When I arrived at the village on Route 96A I found the car in question. Standing by it was the caller, a heavy-set white male with one ear. His fuel truck was parked nearby.

We introduced ourselves. I went to the rear of the vehicle and looked carefully at the trunk. He asked me, "What are you looking for?"

"I'm looking for a bullet hole," I replied.

He mentioned that a fellow home from the U.S. Army might be the person I was looking for. He told me how to get to a farm where the fellow might be staying. I radioed State Police Waterloo, the Zone Headquarters, and requested a tow truck to impound the abandoned brown Chevrolet Convertible bearing no plates. I waited for the tow truck to arrive.

It didn't take me long to locate the farmhouse. The yard was full of old junk cars and the place seemed run-down. No one appeared to be around. It was an eerie place.

I looked in one of the cars parked against a large maple tree. Sleeping in the back seat was a white male wearing a khaki uniform. The shirt was torn, and the fellow looked very dishevelled. To me it looked like the fellow I had briefly observed in my headlights at the gas station. He appeared to be in his mid-twenties and quite muscular.

The training academy had always preached about self-discipline, and this lesson was imbedded in my mind. Then I thought, what will this guy do when I wake him up? "Wake up, fellow". I said in a loud bass voice.

"Wha,— What? he replied groggily.

I told him that he would have been smart if he had pulled the car over instead of trying to outrun me.

He identified himself, and I told him he was under arrest for at least eight violations of the Vehicle and Traffic Law: They were speeding, reckless driving, failure to keep right, passing a red light, no operator's license, unregistered motor vehicle, operating without insurance, and failing to comply with the request of a police officer.

En route to the office of the Justice of the Peace, the handcuffed prisoner remained mute. The special file check with Troop Headquarters revealed that he was a deserter from the U.S. Army.

The defendant entered a plea of guilty to all charges and was committed to the Seneca County Jail in lieu of $1200.00 in fines.

When I returned to the Ovid barracks I contacted the military authorities at Sampson Air Force Base, and in turn they contacted the military police at Fort Deavens, Massachusetts, regarding the deserter.

The apprehension of this person gave me a feeling of accomplishment. I asked myself, "Why did he desert from the military service and why did he display a deviant behavior?" If he had only pulled over when he knew he was being pursued, it possibly would have had a much different conclusion.

On the Monday morning following my arrest of the deserter, I was sitting at the desk in the Ovid barracks when the telephone rang. It was the Lieutenant from Zone Headquarters. He told me to proceed to Waterloo forthwith. I asked him what it was all about, and he assured me that we would discuss the matter in his office.

While en route to Zone Headquarters I couldn't help but wonder what difficulty was facing me. I parked my troop car in the barracks lot and went into the office.

Sergeant Lawrence Fox was sitting behind his desk. I didn't get a chance to say hello before he informed me, "The Lieutenant will see you now."

I entered the Lieutenant's office and gave him a brisk hand salute. I was greeted by the Lieutenant with the words, "Hello, stupid." "What did you call me?" I replied.

The Lieutenant then told me to sign a paper lying on the top of the desk. I looked at the document and saw it was a typed resignation. "Sign it! Sign it!" He repeated in an authoritative tone of voice.

I told the Lieutenant eyeball to eyeball. "I'm not signing this paper or any other paper for you or anyone else." I paused. "Furthermore, Lieutenant, I am no more stupid than you are. Do you understand me?" I spoke loudly.

He flashed back, "You can't talk to me like that. I'm a Lieutenant." Then he added sternly, "You didn't notify us about the discharge of a firearm."

"Even my father doesn't talk to me that way, and I know one thing for certain: you are not my father." I wondered if this man talked to his son this way, if he had one.

I then asked the Lieutenant to come outside behind the barracks so we could settle it. I had never been addressed by anyone as I was that late summer morning of 1954. I realize now that I should have kept my mouth shut, but I felt I was correct. He, of course, refused.

The Lieutenant dismissed me and told me to proceed to Ovid and pack my gear for I was being transferred to Waterloo for close supervision. The Lieutenant informed me he would take the matter up with the Troop Commander. I left the office and went to the Ovid barracks.

The foot locker was again taken out of the attic and packed with all my gear. The faithful Plymouth was again loaded and, after leaving a note for Trooper Spanbauer, I left for my new barracks. I wondered what was in store for me now!

By the time I arrived at Waterloo a teletype message had been received which indicated I had been transferred. I was told by the Sergeant that the matter between the Lieutenant and me had been concluded by the Lieutenant's telephone call to the Troop Commander. I was not being fired, and my punishment for not filing a discharge of firearms report was two weeks of confinement to the desk at Waterloo. This was considered mild punishment.

The Sergeant told me that the man that I had talked with in Interlaken, James Hill, had called the Lieutenant and told him that I was on my knees looking for a bullet hole the back of the Chevrolet convertible that the deserter had abandoned. From that day on I always kept my eyes open for the potential "back stabber."

A few days after the incident I went into the Lieutenant's office and told him, apologetically, that my conduct had been somewhat unprofessional. I certainly did not want any trouble with him.

The two weeks went by at a slow pace, but they were a learning experience, too. I became acquainted with the Waterloo district and especially with the three-lane "killer highway" between Waterloo and Geneva. While confined to desk duty, many telephone calls were received from citizens reporting numerous fatal and serious personal injury accidents along the "killer highway."

Our patrols watched Route 5 and 20 very closely because of the three lanes and the fatal and personal injuries that occurred frequently.

Sergeant Lawrence F. Fox was the Station Commander and the people under him followed his directives and orders without hesitation. He was a firm supervisor, but fair.

One day at the Waterloo barracks I received a letter from Peggy which contained some astounding news. She told me that if I could find an apartment or house she would move to New York State. This had been the only letter from her in three months. Although love for Peggy was deeply ingrained in my heart, I couldn't help but feel that our relationship was strained and fragile.

I contacted father and mother and told them the good news. Father asked me what I had in mind for a residence. I replied that a mobile home, for a starter, might be a good investment.

I called Peggy and said, "Honey I'm so happy that you're coming to live with me. I've missed you so much."

"I've missed you too. I'm planning on transferring to the New York Telephone Company and I'll explain it further when I get there."

I reminded her that my four-day pass was scheduled a week from now and that I would look at mobile homes the next day. She said she would arrive in New York by Greyhound Bus during my four-day pass. I assured her again that I missed her very much. She said she felt the same.

The following day I went in search of a mobile home for us. Luck was with me! I located a 24-footer at the Waterloo Trailer Sales, which was located near the Green Acre Trailer Park on Route 5 and 20 in the Waterloo patrol area. The salesman was a fine gentleman. He advised me that they had sold many trailers and mobile homes to people in the Green Acre Park. The $1200.00 purchase was finalized, and in two days the trailer was set up in the Green Acre Park all ready for us to move into.

The park, on a slight hill, was neat and clean. I met the owner and he told me that the rent would be due each month, with a ten day grace period before the interest would be applied to the rental fee. He described the services we would enjoy at the park, which included a reading room, a laundry, and a horse-shoe rink.

When I returned to the barracks I told Sergeant Fox that my wife was moving to New York State. He seemed pleased and told me that he would see that I had enough time off duty to get settled. Everything seemed to be in good order at the moment.

On the third day of my four-day pass I drove our Plymouth to the Greyhound terminal in Syracuse. I was very eager to see Peggy after all this time. Almost a year had gone by since we had seen each other. I knew it was a sacrifice for her to change her mind and join me in New York. Leaving her widowed mother and brother was a difficult decision to make. I thought maybe we would have the chance to start all over again for a good relationship in our marriage.

The bus from Springfield was on time. The excitement I felt was beyond words. Peggy was about the fifth person to exit the coach. She was wearing a dark blue suit and carrying a tan raincoat over her arm. She hadn't changed except for gaining a couple of pounds (She weighed about 115). The excitement continued to build in my heart, and I embraced her with a firm hug. We kissed each other warmly. Her Irish smile seemed genuine. I told her I had been waiting for this moment a long, long time.

On the way to our trailer we talked about Julia and Eddie. Peggy assured me that they were fine and told me that Julia had convinced her to move to New York to be with me. She seemed sincere about the move and told me that she had worked out the transfer to the New York Telephone Company. I was happy for both of us.

We stopped at a restaurant outside of Auburn and enjoyed a sandwich, but felt that it was a little too late to bother my parents. We drove on to Waterloo after our snack, to our new home.

I took Peggy's baggage into the small trailer and helped her with the unpacking.

"This trailer seems to be small and there isn't very much room," She said, disappointedly.

"I agree." I replied, sheepishly.

The long separation exploded into a passionate encounter, after which we both fell into a deep sleep of complete solitude.

The arrangement Peggy had made with the New York Telephone Company was a wise one. She would be working for the company at the Sampson Air Force Training Station. Two gentlemen in upper management would be escorting Peggy to work each day. She would be picked up each morning at our trailer park and dropped off each night after work. It was very beneficial for both of us, especially with my police career.

I met both of the gentlemen, and they assured me that Peggy would be safe and secure in her new workplace. Both the telephone executives were in their late fifties and appeared to be true professionals. Peggy and I were both pleased with the arrangement.

The four-day pass ended rapidly. When I reported to work the next day, Sergeant Fox asked me how everything had gone with the move. I told him all seemed fine and that it was wonderful to have my wife close by, even though I had to sleep in the barracks every night except for my two nights a week off, and my monthly four-day pass, and my four weeks' annual leave.

Peggy enjoyed her job at Sampson. I was able to stop by for supper every evening, and each night just before 11:00 p.m. I would stop by the trailer to see if everything was alright. I knew that it would be difficult for her to be alone so much. We had a telephone installed in the event of any type of emergency.

The schedule in the State Troopers was a grueling one. The small salary we Troopers received for working 120 hours a week was an insult for the dedication we gave. In that era people joined the Troopers for the adventure of the occupation. It certainly wasn't for the money.

The shock of my life hit me between the eyes one morning in the Sergeant's office. I had been working exceptionally well, above and beyond what was required. The Sergeant had just given me my duty assignment, when the Lieutenant entered the room with a big grin on his face. He said sarcastically, "I've got some good news for you, Briant."

I quizzically replied, "You have, sir?"

"Yes, I have. You are being transferred to State Police Herkimer in fifteen days." He had a smug expression on his face.

I couldn't believe what this man was saying. I had gone through so much. All the sadness I had held in my heart for my marriage, which just now seemed finally to be improving. My wife had just arrived, and now I was being transferred ninety miles away to another station!

My inner desire was to take this bastard outside the barracks and punch him in his nose. But! I resisted and held back the rage.

This turnabout was just an example of the typical internal workings of any organization. A worker will dedicate him or herself to an employer and work his or her foolish head off, but it is to no avail if the individual does not fit into the profile that an organization dictates.

I strongly sensed that the transfer was initiated by the Lieutenant to discourage me and possibly to persuade me to resign. I wasn't the only one who thought it was a revengeful act. My inner wisdom convinced me that this was a game of personalities in conflict.

Peggy cried when I told her the news. I comforted her the best I could. We had been so content in our effort to pursue our fragile marriage, which would take time to heal. I suggested to her that maybe I should resign and go back to Massachusetts. Then I thought about the Commander of the Infantry outfit who had busted me to Private from Staff Sergeant. It was in that small trailer that I came to a final conclusion: I'll keep my mouth closed and play their infantile game.

The day I left for Herkimer was a sad day. We didn't have enough funds to move the trailer. Peggy really couldn't ask for another transfer from the telephone company. I told her how much I loved her, and we held each other in our arms for a long time. We could actually hear our heartbeats pounding in our chests. It was deeply difficult for us to separate again.

Ninety miles from Waterloo, fifteen miles east of Utica, the quaint Village of Herkimer rests in a valley situated in the county bearing the same name, which stretches northward to Old Forge and south toward the Village of West Winfield on Route 20. The barracks consisted of an older two-story building, yellow in color. Like many of the state police installations throughout New York, the building had been leased by the State for a given period of time.

I pulled into the driveway and parked the car. I sat for a few minutes thinking about Peggy and wondering if she were alright in our small cramped trailer home ninety miles away. The only relatives close to Peggy were my parents in Throopsville. We knew that we could count on them if there was an emergency, but this fact did not ease the pressure and tension that I was encountering in myself. In high school athletics we had all been taught good sportsmanship, and I truly believed in this concept. What the Lieutenant had done to me by this transfer certainly didn't seem to fit the definition of good sportsmanship. My heart was being torn apart, with our marriage still in a state of fragility. I loved being a State Trooper, but this twist of fate was too painfully absurd.

I got out of the Plymouth with some of my gear and headed to the barracks. The first person I met when I went inside was Corporal Lewis Johnson of the Bureau of Criminal Investigation. We shook hands as he welcomed me to the Herkimer barracks. He was a soft-spoken man with heavy dark eyebrows. His voice was gentle, and I could feel his eyes searching my face for a response.

"It is nice to meet you, Corporal," I managed to say.

"John, I will show you where your room is located, and you can start putting your clothes in the closet. Before you do, John, you'd better sign in the station blotter. I will send a teletype to Troop Headquarters that you have reported for duty."

I finished unloading my personal car and placed everything in its proper place. The dresser and closet were full. The footlocker was placed in yet another barracks attic. My name had been entered on the pass schedule, and I noticed that I had the following Wednesday night off, which meant that I could go off-duty at 5:30 on Wednesday evening and report back to the barracks at 10:30 the next morning. I solaced myself with the thought that Peggy would be happy to see me on Wednesday night.

My thoughts were interrupted when Corporal Johnson, accompanied by Sergeant Ray Fogarty, the Station Commander, approached me. The grey-haired Irish Sergeant extended his hand to shake. Our hands were locked in a firm grip. He smiled and said, "Welcome to Herkimer, Trooper."

There were three other uniform Troopers assigned to Herkimer, and another BCI man. I met them all within the following week. They all seemed very nice, and it was apparent they enjoyed their position of Trooper. Very seldom did we have everybody working at the same time; someone would be on night pass or a four-day pass or annual leave. Many times there were only two of us working from 7:00 AM to 11:00 PM. We had no night patrol running out of the Herkimer barracks, and any calls that came in after 11:00 PM. would be handled by one of us. We took turns on the after-11:00 PM calls. Most of our night calls were from a weigh station just outside Little Falls.

During this period of time in the mid-fifties the weigh station was manned twenty-four hours a day. The violations that they discovered generally dealt with overweight trucks. A truck driver would pull his truck (a straight-job or semi-trailer outfit) onto the scales, and the total gross weight was determined in seconds. There were also drivers without chauffeur licenses, or log books not properly maintained. The weigh station brought us many violations as well as sleepless nights.

The State Troopers were the primary law enforcement agency in the region. During those years The Herkimer County Sheriff's Department did not have a road patrol; however, they maintained the jail and served civil papers. We enjoyed a good relationship with the sheriff's department, and all the small village police departments in Herkimer County. During my tenure at the Herkimer barracks many adventurous incidents took place.

One particular case happened while I was doing desk duty. I was the only Trooper working that afternoon. I heard the station radio as it broadcast a stolen car alarm. The radio transmission from Troop Headquarters at Oneida described the car, its color, the dealer plate, and even the car thief. Their broadcast went to all our stations throughout Troop "D". The broadcast indicated that the thief might be en route to the Little Falls area.

I made the proper entry on the station radio log, got up from the desk, and strolled over to our large front window, which gave our barracks a clear view of Route 5. About twenty minutes went by, and then I spotted the car described in the radio broadcast.

I hurriedly grabbed my stetson and ran out of the barracks to the parked troop car in the front parking lot. I burned rubber when I left the parking lot. The road between Herkimer and Little Falls was curvy and hilly. I floored the 1953 Ford Troop Car, and the speedometer indicator lurched ahead to 80 or 85 miles per hour. I couldn't see the wanted car ahead of me until I was halfway to Little Falls. I put the siren on and pulled alongside. The operator was a young white male wearing glasses. I pointed to him to pull over. He did not respond and kept on driving. Oncoming traffic forced me to pull in back of him.

I pulled alongside for the second time, only this time I displayed my .45 Caliber revolver. He looked over toward me and apparently realized that I meant business. He pulled the stolen car off the road and stopped. I told the twenty-seven-year old that he was under arrest for Grand Larceny/auto theft. The handcuffs fastened to his wrists induced him to reveal all the details of the car theft. He also told me his driver's license in New York State had been revoked.

When I pulled into the barracks yard I parked the Troop Car and took my prisoner into the station. During my pursuit of the individual I had radioed Troop Headquarters and advised them of the situation and the apprehension. Trooper Stanley Ralton had just returned from a special detail and was sitting at the desk.

"John", he said, "I see that you have been busy while I was away."

"That's the way it goes sometimes Stan." I grinned.

The car thief was arrested on a Vehicle and Traffic Misdemeanor, Driving while license revoked, and arraigned before the local Town Justice, who imposed a twenty-five dollar fine which was paid by the defendant. He was held at the barracks until the officers arrived from the City of Oneida. The defendant was returned to Oneida to answer to the charge of Grand Larceny/Auto in that criminal jurisdiction.

I didn't receive a medal for the apprehension of the stolen car. My reward was my self satisfaction in doing the job that I was sworn to do.

After the defendant had left the barracks with the Oneida policemen, Stan and I talked about the case. We commented to one another about the attitude of the defendant. The guy had conducted himself as a gentleman all during the process of apprehension and arraignment. We discussed the fact that it could have gone the other way if he had been armed. This apprehension was the kind that policemen prefer, without violence. It worked out well.

Another apprehension made without incident was of a fourteen-year-old boy and a seventeen-year-old girl in a stolen car in Poland. A filling station operator called the Herkimer barracks reporting that two people stopped for gasoline and drove off without paying for the gas. When I was called on the radio from the Herkimer barracks I advised them that I was located between the Village of Herkimer and Middleville. I pulled off to the side of the road and waited. It was only a few minutes before the wanted car passed.

My investigation revealed that the two young people had stolen the car in Williamsport, Pennsylvania, from a used car lot. They had then proceeded to a parking lot of a plant in Pennsylvania and stolen a Pennsylvania plate. They had then driven to Utica, into a hospital parking lot, and stolen a set of New York State plates from a car that belonged to a patient in the hospital. They had placed the Pennsylvania plate from their stolen car under the front seat and installed the stolen New York plates on the car. When apprehended, the fourteen-year-old boy admitted the theft.

The Pennsylvania authorities were notified and came to Herkimer to return the boy and girl to their jurisdiction. They informed us that the young boy had been involved in numerous car thefts in Pennsylvania. The filling station operator did not recover his funds for the stolen gasoline, but the successful conclusion of this case was the result of his telephone call to the Troopers.

There was constant activity in the Herkimer patrol area. I met many wonderful people during my tenure there. It was the close cooperation of the citizens in the community that brought many cases to my attention and to the attention of other station members. I loved my work. In my estimation there is no other job like that of being a New York State Trooper. On the street and highways is where the job is. The element of helping is crucial to being a successful officer. He or she has to treat the citizens with respect and dignity. There should be no place for a bully in the police profession.

My night off twice a week, my four-day pass once a month, and my twenty-eight annual leave days brought me home to Peggy. It was a tiring drive to Waterloo during these times, but I was always happy to see my wife. We would usually go out to eat when I came home. We visited with my parents as often as we could. It was during one of those visits home when Peggy became pregnant. We were so happy! Peggy continued her work with the telephone company, and the two executives with whom she rode back and forth to work kept her spirits up.

I was shocked! Just when I thought everything was looking up. I had been told that I would be leaving Herkimer for a barracks closer to Waterloo. I left Herkimer to man the midnight tour of duty in the communications room at Oneida about two nights a week. I was required to report at midnight and work until eight o'clock in the morning. This work schedule went on for about three weeks. It was about all I could stand. I hadn't entered the Troopers to be a communication specialist!

Today such treatment would be called harassment, but back in the fifties it was veiled as job experience. I knew in my heart that the Lieutenant in Waterloo was still trying to impress me with his power.

One day yet another teletype message was received at Herkimer, the same as the ones that had preceded it: "Trooper Briant will report for Teletype duty at 12:00 midnight."

It was all I could stand. I called the New Hartford Lieutenant and told him that I would like to have a conference with him. The Lieutenant advised me that he would meet me at Herkimer the same day.

Lieutenant Melvin Handville was a tall man, about six foot five inches. He almost had to duck when he came through a doorway. Lieutenant Handville listened to me. I told him that it was apparent to me that someone wanted me to resign. I told him who I thought it was. I explained to him about my frustrations and my fragile marriage. I told him of my devoted love for the State Troopers and what the job meant to me. He listened, and listened some more, as I vented my anger about an entirely different type of Lieutenant.

Lieutenant Handville gave me encouragement. He told me to report to the communications section as directed this time. He urged me not to resign. "Report to Troop Headquarters and I'll see what I can do about getting you relieved of that type of duty." he said with understanding.

"Yes, Sir, I will." I left the room feeling somewhat encouraged.

Within four hours another teletype message was received: "Trooper Briant disregard reporting to Troop Headquarters date." —by the authority of the Troop Commander.

To this day I do not know what Lieutenant Handville said or did, but whatever it was, it worked.

The drive back and forth to Waterloo was very tiring even for a twenty-five-year-old Trooper. It was on one of my night passes that Peggy told me the good news. It had been confirmed that she was pregnant. Both of us were overjoyed with the thought of having a baby. We didn't care if it were a girl or a boy, as long as it was healthy.

The work activity was continuous at Herkimer. During deer season of 1955, Corporal Johnson became involved in a complex hunting-accident investigation. It was an educational experience to observe this veteran BCI Corporal seek out the facts in the case, which involved seven men who were all friends and all hunting deer together. A deer had been spotted by the hunters and they had all fired at it; however, one of their party was struck by a rifle shot and later died.

To determine who fired the fatal shot, all the deer rifles had to be confiscated. They were tagged and transported to the State Police Laboratory in Albany. The laboratory examination determined which rifle the fatal shot had been fired from. Corporal Johnson took sworn statements from the entire hunting party, each affidavit describing what each hunter had observed and how each had fired upon the deer.

The case was presented to the Herkimer County Grand Jury. The man who fired the fatal shot was indicted for Criminal Negligent Homicide while engaged in the act of hunting. It was a tragic accident, not only for the victim, but for the family of the deceased and his other friends who were on that hunt.

Another tragedy occurred about the same time when an elderly man took his nephew on a hunt. They had prearranged to meet in the woods near a spring. The nephew arrived earlier at the meeting spot and sat down behind a tree. The uncle approached from another direction, saw an object near a tree, and fired, thinking it was a fox. Instead, his shot caused serious injury to his nephew when the bullet tore through the younger man's left knee.

I was assigned to this case and arrested the older man for Criminal Negligence which caused injury to another person while engaged in the act of hunting. He was convicted and spent time in the Herkimer County Jail. The uncle never hunted again, to my knowledge, and the nephew had a stiff left leg for the rest of his life.

Every effort was made prior to hunting season to inform sportsmen that gun safety is very important to everyone. This is accomplished through the various media sources; radio, television, and newspapers. It only takes a second to be injured or possibly lose or take a life. This is an ongoing policy of law enforcement throughout the nation.

Burglaries of homes, camps, and businesses are a continuing problem. During my tenure at the Herkimer barracks almost every burglary case was closed by an arrest. Again we had to thank Corporal Johnson of the BCI. During his many years of service in the area he had learned well the deviant attitude that a small percentage of the citizens held. He could almost name the burglar for a particular crime. He unselfishly shared important information with us and assisted us with each case until it was closed. Many of us benefited from working with a man of this high caliber.

One night the telephone rang at State Police Herkimer, and the caller was the man who owned the Trailer Park in Waterloo. He told me that Peggy had been taken to a local hospital, with an apparent miscarriage.

I obtained permission to leave immediately and rushed home to Waterloo. Peggy was in the Seneca Falls Hospital. She had lost our child. My guts were in pain and tears flowed down my cheeks as I gazed at her in the hospital bed. She looked pale and sad. I comforted her well into the next day and stayed home for a few days on emergency leave. My parents, when contacted, showed their concern. I couldn't help but think that if I had been closer to home, possibly the miscarriage could have been averted.

Peggy took some sick leave time off from the New York Telephone Company to recuperate. Reluctantly I went back to duty at the Herkimer barracks.

All the fellows at the Herkimer barracks told me they were sorry to hear of Peggy's miscarriage. I became a little depressed, upset by the fact that being ninety miles from our modest trailer home was an added burden to our relationship as husband and wife.

I soon was diverted from the depressed state, however when one morning I answered a call about an accident which occurred just east of the barracks on Route 5 near the Nestle's Plant. Several people were seriously hurt. When I arrived at the scene I tended to the injured. The Valley Ambulance Service arrived, and Connie Nowacki, a former Trooper turned ambulance owner and operator, came to my assistance.

A westbound car had crossed over a double line and struck an eastbound car almost head on. All the injured were cared for and taken to the Herkimer Hospital. The roadway was cleared. A routine personal injury accident, the reader might conclude? Not by any means. This particular accident investigation was part of my life for five years, and still today I think about it and the harassment that I as the investigating Trooper had to endure.

The westbound car was owned and had been operated by a law student. He had received a serious injury to one of his legs, and in fact I rendered first aid to him first as it looked nasty. He healed.

He was arrested for reckless driving and pled not guilty. He pursued his case to the Court of Claims, bringing a lawsuit against the State of New York and against me as an agent for the State. As I said it went on for five years. I was subpoenaed on several occasions. Who served the subpoena on those occasions? None other than the law student, now an attorney.

The climax of the case came in the Court of Claims in Utica. I was cross-examined fiercely. In the front row of the court were approximately twenty-five young attorneys attempting to intimidate me with icy stares, evidently colleagues of the plaintiff. It was certainly a good training session for any Trooper.

You could have heard a pin drop when the Court of Claims Justice arose to speak, in his flowing black robes. "Now in this matter of———— ——— vs. The People of the State of New York." He went on to state, "Mr.———— ——— I am most impressed with the brief you have prepared in this matter." The Justice went on to say that he would read the brief and would take it under consideration, but the issue here was the validity of the instruments which included the information, the deposition and the duly issued warrant of arrest. The Justice's words still ring in my ears today: "I find that the instruments stand as they are. They had no flaws in them."

Prior to the proceedings I had been sarcastically summoned to Troop Headquarters, while an officer, hovered over me, and read the bill of particulars to me, and told me that I was in trouble. I often think about that moment. Then I smile as I recall the words of the Court of Claims Justice.

A few weeks later an article appeared in the Utica area paper relative to the case. The Court of Claims ruled "No cause for action"— case dismissed.

I will let the reader imagine the momentum of the case and the dollar signs that appeared in the dreams of this intellectual law student as he indicated to many of the citizens of my patrol area how he was going to teach that "Trooper" a lesson.

The salary of a State Trooper during the 1950's was supplemented by a food allowance of $4.25 per day. This amount covered the member's three meals each day. This allowance did not afford you the finest food served in local diners or restaurants. It was difficult to sustain the proper dietary intake to sustain oneself.

Another Trooper and I were invited to dinner by a family in Herkimer. That late summer day the telephone rang as we were about to sit down to eat. The phone call alerted us to the fact that a New York Central Train had derailed. We quickly thanked our hosts and left for the scene.

When we arrived we learned that forty cars of an eighty-three-car-train had left the tracks. They included box cars and gasoline tank cars. No one had been injured. One of the large pillars supporting the New York State Thruway bridge had been struck, but withstood the impact. The exact location of the derailment occurred on Kay's curve one-half mile west of Herkimer. The cars were piled up like cord wood. The vehicular traffic was in a snarl for a long period of time. We sent a File 3 Teletype message to Troop and Division Headquarters describing the accident in detail. The derailment had been caused by a wheel breaking on one of the gondola cars.

It was a miracle that no one was injured. This was my first railroad accident investigation, but during my tenure at the Herkimer barracks there were several train car accidents. Most of these occurred at the Deerfield Crossing located west of Herkimer.

One evening I was on routine patrol in the Newport and Middleville area, north of Herkimer. The Herkimer barracks called me on the Troop car radio and advised me to return.

When I arrived at the barracks I learned the reason for the call. A prison disturbance was taking place at the Great Meadow Correctional Institution located at Comstock.

The demonstration had started on a Wednesday evening when the inmates staged a sit-down strike in the recreational yard, allegedly in protest against the shortening of the recreational period by five minutes. In the early hours of the demonstration, no violence had occurred; there had only been some hollering and yelling in the area.

At the Herkimer barracks I was advised to pack a small bag of shaving gear and prepare to leave for Comstock.

It was approximately 9:30 p.m. when three troop cars, each carrying five Troopers, rolled out of the Herkimer barracks for the Comstock area. These young, rugged Troopers would soon experience the turmoil of a prison disturbance. We had taken our barracks rifles, which were the old Winchesters with the saddle ring located on the left side of the breech. All of us were a little excited and apprehensive as to what we would be facing.

The trip to Great Meadow Correctional Facility had taken us about three hours. We arrived at the prison just before midnight. When I got out of the Troop car I couldn't help but think of Peggy, Julia, and Eddie. I thought about my parents and Joan and David, too. The Sergeant at Herkimer had promised me that he would call Peggy to let her know of our hurried departure.

The fifteen of us from Troop "D" met other Troopers from all over the State. We all assembled in the prison dining room to await further instructions.

New York State Correction Commissioner Thomas J. McHugh rushed to the prison from St. Lawrence University, where he had been attending a conference on crime and juvenile delinquency.

It was a tense situation when Commissioner McHugh spoke to the rioters over the institution's loudspeaker. He said, "If you return to your cells, I will arrange to talk to your leaders. There is no commitment, no promise, no bargain. If you do not return, we're going to put you in there and we have the power to do it. You have five minutes to make up your minds." he declared. "Drop all weapons. Move out twenty at a time with hands behind your heads. This is an ultimatum."

The prisoners failed to move from the northeast corner of the recreational area, where they huddled together. McHugh counted the five minutes over the loudspeaker, and then the battle begun.

The force of Correction Officers and Troopers moved into the yard. Some carried rifles and others carried batons. The battle was fierce for about one-half-hour.

I remember well the large inmate who came head-on toward me. He held a stick high, ready to strike me, just as I side-stepped and brought him down with a baton blow to the left shinbone below the knee. His part of the disturbance had concluded. There was gunfire, and later I learned that two Troopers and a Correctional Officer had been wounded in the melee.

The inmates were lined up in groups of twenty and marched to their cells. The injured inmates were taken to the institution medical facility and given aid.

I was not privy to the interviews that were conducted with the rebellious leaders. I had been a Trooper for only a little over a year and a half. I did learn that many of the inmates whom we encountered were from the New York City area and were serving time for pushing drugs in the inner city.

All of us Troopers were locked in for about three days to insure stability within the prison. In need of baths and shaves after the locked in period, we were each cared for by the individual guards. They took us to their homes; fed us; furnished us with shaving cream, toothpaste, soap and towels; and treated us like family members. The cooperation was excellent.

We were maintained in the Comstock area for a few days until it was evident that the prison remained calm. Some good friendships were made with the Correction Officers during our stay in Comstock.

Little did I know that I would become involved in another prison disturbance many years later. It was during the Attica Prison riot, as a member of the BCI, I was assigned to a special detail investigating the Attica disturbance with other members of the State Police.

The return trip to Herkimer was at a little slower pace than our trip to the institution. We all talked about our combat experience. We were all concerned about our two Troopers who had been wounded, as well as the Correction Officer. It was not until sometime afterward that we learned that all the wounded officers recovered and returned to normal duties. The prison had given us an experience that none of us would forget for a long period of time.

When we returned to our respective stations, our pass list noted we were off-duty for the next two days. I was anxious to see Peggy.

The Plymouth seemed to know the way to Waterloo as I headed westward on the thruway. It was a pleasure to drive on this highway; there were no red lights between Herkimer and Waterloo.

Peggy was waiting for me. She asked me about the prison disturbance and felt sorrow in her heart for our two wounded Troopers and the Correction Officer. We dined out at a Waterloo restaurant that evening and talked almost all night,— well, almost all night. Difficult for both of us were the long periods of time apart and all the frustration that went along with them.

We visited my mother and father. Peggy always maintained contact through the mail with her mother and brother. I knew deep in my heart how she must have missed Holyoke in those lonely days of the mid-fifties.

While on pass we went to look at a new car, a 1954 Mercury sports coupe. We decided to trade the 1953 Plymouth for the Mercury. We arranged to pick up the car on my forthcoming four-day pass. We were young and wanted to spend the little money we had saved. I thought that after Peggy's miscarriage, a new car would cheer her up.

The return trip to the Herkimer barracks was uneventful. When I arrived I checked my mail folder located in the filing cabinet and found that I had received a letter from my brother David. He told me that he had been drafted into the U.S. Army and would shortly be leaving for Fort Dix, New Jersey. He indicated he would like to see me before his departure date. David worked for the General Electric Company in Utica, which was about seventy-six miles from Waterloo.

I sent David a note telling him that my four-day pass would start in a few days and we would get together.

Lieutenant Melvin Handville called me on the telephone the same day and advised me that I was going to be transferred to the LaFayette Barracks in December 1955. He told me that I would be in LaFayette for about three months and then return to the Waterloo area. I happily thanked him for the good news. He said a teletype would be forthcoming.

I was on desk duty at the Herkimer barracks one morning. Anyone sitting at the station desk had a clear vision of the highway and entrance into the barracks parking area. I looked up and saw an officer's car drive in. In a couple of minutes the front door opened. It wasn't Lieutenant Handville.

It was the stone face of the Waterloo Lieutenant. His sour expression broke into an even sourer smirk. "Hello, Briant," he Said.

"It is Trooper Briant, Lieutenant," I shot back.

"Trooper Briant, while Lieutenant Handville is on pass, I was called to fill in for him, and I'm out inspecting Zone 1 today." The Lieutenant went on to say, "Trooper Briant, I do not have any hard feelings toward you in any way. I just wanted to let you know this."

"I understand, Lieutenant. However, my wife and I have gone

through a great deal of hardship with the transfer and her miscarriage. Sir, I'm really not interested whether you have ill feelings toward me or not." I said sharply. My jaw tightened as I looked him squarely in the face.

I didn't say another word, for I knew that it wouldn't take too much to really get into hot water with this callous individual.

The Lieutenant checked the casebook and numerous station files. He looked around the barracks. He finally signed through the station blotter and left the building.

I looked across the room and out through the large window as his troop car turned right out of the driveway.

I hoped that I hadn't rekindled the agitation for this man dormant in myself for a long time. I went back to my report writing.

Sergeant Fogarty had been transferred, and Sergeant Fred Sargenti was the uniform Sergeant in charge of the barracks. Sergeant Sargenti's hometown was Auburn, New York. Like Fogarty he was a very intelligent man with many years of service in the Troopers. Sometimes Sergeant John C. Miller from the New Hartford barracks would pull relief duty at Herkimer. The Sergeants and the Troopers with whom I had the privilege to work during the year of 1955 were men of integrity.

I learned a great deal from BCI Corporal Lew Johnson. As I previously indicated, he was a methodical investigator. He didn't rush, and when he built a case against a villain, a conviction was forthcoming.

Lieutenant Handville was on target. The file 14 Teletype message came. The message read: "Trooper Briant transferred to SP LaFayette, NY effective December 30th, 1955." I looked at the teletype for a long time. I wanted to make certain that it was authentic.

In the mid-fifties any Trooper or member that was assigned to a particular patrol area would in that period of time touch the lives of many people. My tenure at SP Herkimer was no exception. The businesspeople, the government workers, the citizens whom I met during that time in my police career will always be held in a private file in my heart. I could have stayed in Herkimer for the rest of my career, but down deep I knew that I had to get on with my life and Peggy, and, of course, more police work.

I would be remiss if I didn't include in my recollections the young people in the Herkimer area: the grammar school children, the high school children and the young men and women who went on to college to capture higher plateaus of education. Even in 1955 the young people were our most important resource. One could say that one of the unwritten rules for a Trooper was to help our youth pass through adolescence without too many bumps and bruises.

The day of departure from Herkimer was a cold one. My personal car sputtered as I turned right out of the barracks and headed west for a four-day pass and Peggy. As I left the driveway I tooted my horn, bidding farewell to the Troopers standing by the front door. My memories of Herkimer will always be unique.

The ninety miles to Waterloo were the same miles that I had covered so many times.

When I pulled into the Green Acre Trailer Park I saw our trailer lights on. The Christmas decorations were still intact. Peggy opened the door, and at last I could spend four days with my wife before reporting to the LaFayette barracks.

The four-day pass was busy for Peggy and me. We went to Syracuse and found an apartment. The rent for a one-bedroom apartment at the Onondaga Garden Apartments was $110.00 per month, including heat and water. The electricity was to be paid by the lessee. We signed a year's lease. Our soon-to-be home was located on the second floor at 127 Ford Avenue.

While in Syracuse we stopped at Fiegel Trailer Sales and made arrangements to sell our Waterloo trailer home for $500.00. Fiegel's told us they would go to Waterloo and tow the trailer to their lot in Syracuse. We were happy with the arrangements.

Peggy had already spoken with her supervisor at Sampson Air Force Training Station, and she put in for a transfer to the Syracuse office of the New York Telephone Company. Things seemed to be going our way for a change.

I had talked with First Sergeant William Keeley, and he had assured me that if I liked the LaFayette area, it would not be necessary for me to return to the Waterloo barracks. I thanked Sergeant Keeley for his interest in our welfare and told him that I would continue to exert all my effort to perform my duties to the best of my ability.

I reported to Lafayette for duty the day after my four-day pass. The Corporal in charge of the barracks was William McDermott. The BCI Corporal was James Cerino. Troopers Stanley Kogut and Neil Belmont were the rest of the barracks personnel. They all greeted me with

"Welcome to LaFayette."

"Gentlemen, I'm glad to be here," I replied.

The barracks was a three-bedroom ranch. The two offices were located in the front of the bedrooms. It was a patrol station and did not have a teletype machine. All teletype messages and assignments were directed from North Syracuse, the Zone 2 Headquarters. Two uniform troop cars and one BCI troop car, (all Fords) were assigned to the barracks. U.S. Route 20, as well as U.S. Route 11, passed through the LaFayette patrol area. Parallel to Route 11 was Route 11A, which ran through the Onondaga Indian Reservation. Route 80 started at the south side of the City of Syracuse and ran south and then east toward New Woodstock.

In the assigned patrol area were the hamlets of Nedrow, South Onondaga, Vesper, Apulia, Apulia Station, Delphi Falls, Pompey, and LaFayette, and the villages of Tully and Fabius. The approximate population in the patrol area was 26,000 citizens. The population of the Onondaga Indian Reservation was approximately 1,240 citizens. The Reservation was a part of our patrol area.

The area was mostly agricultural and residential. The land area was a mixture of hills, valleys, and flat land. It was very scenic in each of the seasons.

The first day on duty at LaFayette was filled with administrative information that I needed to know. I was assigned a bedroom with Neil Belmont. A mail folder was inserted in the top filing drawer of the filing cabinet located in the uniform office. I was informed by Corporal McDermott that I was the rookie Trooper at LaFayette and would be so listed in order of seniority.

The patrol station was usually staffed by at least two Troopers at any one time. There was someone on a pass day, a four day pass, or annual leave. Again my footlocker was placed in the barracks attic. My uniforms were hung in the closet of my assigned bedroom. The dresser was filled with socks, underwear, handkerchiefs, and my memorandum holder for policy memos which came down from Division Headquarters and Troop Headquarters.

In January 1956 Peggy was transferred to the East Fayette Street New York Telephone Company office. Our apartment was settled with brand-new medium-priced furniture. Because the apartment was located on the south side of Syracuse, it was usually possible for me to have the evening meal at home with Peggy; I was within one mile of my assigned district.

Corporal McDermott assigned me to the patrol area between the City of Syracuse southern limits to U.S. Route 20. Even though I was not restricted to that area, it was my official assigned district from 1956 to 1960. When a Trooper is assigned to a patrol area, he or she becomes familiar with just about every person who resides therein.

When I first arrived at LaFayette I took turns riding with the Corporal and Troopers Kogut and Belmont. I soon learned the territory, which consisted of 662 square miles. I met all the town supervisors, town highway superintendents, Niagara Mohawk Power people, ambulance services, volunteer fire department members, restaurant owners, and bar room owners. Each of the towns had at least two Justices of the Peace.

The district had a mixed blend of activity. There were always auto accidents occurring. Some were fatal and some were personal injury accidents, while others were fender benders. Usually a traffic summons would be issued to the person who caused the accident. There were many deer/car accidents.

Not only auto accidents prevailed. The area's many farms initiated accidents usually involving death or serious personal injury. An accident of this description occurred in the Town of Pompey in 1956 when a small child was killed as he went through a hay baler. It was a terrible death for the child as well as a tragedy for the family members. In another accident a farm worker lost his right arm up to the elbow in a corn cutter. Another farmer became entangled in the power take-off unit on his tractor and was seriously injured. Most of the time this type of accident was carelessness on the part of the worker.

Even the most seasoned Trooper has a difficult time investigating accidents where bodies are mutilated, even those Troopers who have served in military combat and have been exposed to death and injury. It is a part of the job that we are sworn to perform.

During the winter months the district is exposed to many snowstorms. In the hills near Pompey, the north and south county highways are swept with strong winds, causing many areas along each highway where drivers are blinded by the blowing snow. Numerous skiers en route to the ski slopes have been seriously injured on these highways. Many times, only one Trooper was on duty in those years, and alone would go from accident to accident until they were all investigated.

A Trooper in those years, working 120 hours a week, could expect to be away from home the majority of the time. Residing in the barracks made it especially difficult for the married Trooper and his family. Only on the four-day passes or annual leave could he actually spend good family time at home. It was not until 1960 that the Troopers would experience a reduction in the work week.

At a patrol station such as LaFayette, when the Trooper came off patrol at 11:00 p.m. he would sign in the station blotter with his activities that occurred from his 7:00 a.m. to 11:00 p.m. shift. The long days on patrol were grueling, and even the young rugged individuals were ready to retire to the bedroom. At LaFayette we had chipped in and purchased a television set. Sometimes we would watch the late news and possibly a movie before retiring. And with no night patrol, we would be responsible for all complaint calls that came in after 11:00 p.m..

An example of the kind of calls we received during the night could be a domestic complaint, arising when a husband stopped at a tavern and upon arriving home got into a fight with his spouse. These were very sensitive complaints to respond to. Sometimes the wife of the intoxicated and disorderly husband would have second thoughts about having her husband arrested, and when he was being placed in the troop car she might even attack the Trooper. Great care and caution in handling this type of complaint was, and is, most essential.

Accidents that occurred after midnight could very well have an intoxicated driver at the wheel. In these cases, not only did a Trooper have to concern himself with the investigation, but possibly defend himself from an arm-swinging drunk who imagines you to be an enemy or intruder. Again, the lone Trooper has always been required to exhibit good common sense in handling the situation.

Not all of our complaints came via the telephone. Many people would stop at our barracks and ring the front doorbell. The seriousness of the complaint would determine whether the bell was rung casually with one or two ding-dongs or rapidly with ding-dongs in fast succession. A rapid ringing usually indicated a serious matter.

It is here that I would like to emphasize that it takes a long time for a Trooper to become seasoned. Just having a badge and gun doesn't necessarily mean that a person knows all the facets of police work. A

Trooper or any police officer is only as good as the people he or she serves. I am not saying that everyone was an angel in the LaFayette area or in any other patrol area of the fifties. The message I am sending here is that during that time there was a very small percent of the masses that possessed, or at least portrayed, an attitude of deviancy.

Pay raises came as increments each year up to seven years of continuous service. The paychecks of Troopers ran well behind that of people involved with industrial jobs. The pay was low, but steady, and for the risk you faced every day of his or her career a Trooper was not properly compensated. It was a profession to which a person had to be dedicated. Although I could probably have earned more in the private sector, I opted to pursue the career of my boyhood dreams.

Most of our daily meals were eaten in local restaurants and diners. The Marybelle located near Tully and Campbell's Diner on the south side of Syracuse were places that served reasonably priced meals. Many of our friends and contacts over the years evolved from our visits at mealtimes. Good food, good natured chatter. And if there were anything going on in the district, we would hear about it during our stops.

During my four-day pass each month and my annual leave, I would take over the duties of executive chef in our small, modest home. Peggy's experience in the culinary department lacked sophistication. She could boil potatoes and grill hamburg or hot dogs, but the early days of our marriage were a learning process for her in the confines of the kitchen. During the longer passes and vacation periods, we sat down to roast of beef, roast turkey, and baked ham. She was more than willing for me to take over the kitchen and display some of the U.S. Air Force know-how. My only problem was that I couldn't help preparing enough food for the whole neighborhood!

Memories of those moments still flash through my mind. I recall the garnishing of those fancy dishes, and those special corned beef sandwiches infiltrated with Russian dressing, and the tasty tangy dill pickles, and the cold draft beer pulsating from the bottom of the thin glasses which had been frosted in the freezer. Those pass days and annual leaves were really the prime time for a Trooper who spent the majority of his time confined to barracks life.

The year 1956 rushed by with several achievements in my life. Finally Peggy and I had the true start of a marriage with hope for the future.

And on the State Trooper side of ledger, I had become very familiar with the LaFayette patrol district; the road locations and where all the Town Justices lived. I had been introduced to key people in the area by the Corporal and met many on my own. Strategically located south of the City of Syracuse and at the intersection of Routes 11 and 20, LaFayette had a constant flow of traffic heading east, west, south and north.

The Onondaga Indian Reservation, located just south of the Hamlet of Nedrow on Route 11A, was of special interest to me. I remembered the many times that my father took me with him to the reservation, when in the early forties he showed movies to the Indian population. My father knew many of the chiefs and clan mothers. I was only twelve in those days, but I remember how friendly the people were to father and me.

Now here I was, fourteen years later, a Trooper patrolling the same reservation. Many of the older Indian people remembered my father and the skinny kid who sat watching the Royal Canadian Mounties on the screen doing battle with the Indians in the far north of Canadian Territories. Yes! I remembered the Onondagas' war whoop around the room as the 16-millimeter camera clicked off the scenes of simulated gunfire depicting the wars of Indians and Mounties.

Many of the homes on the reservation didn't have cellars, but instead were built on a slab of concrete or the dirt soil. Some of them were well kept, while others appeared to be in a run-down condition.

The Onondaga Indian Reservation had a school, which held classes from K to sixth grade. The principal was Ethel VanWie, who started young in her career of teaching at the reservation. She was a graceful lady with a caring concern for the children and their families. I got to know Ethel over the years. She was an unique educator who possessed deep compassion for people.

The reservation also had their own volunteer fire department. They not only responded to all the reservation fires, but were known to assist other area fire fighters if the need arose. They also responded to any serious accident occurring on the reserve.

In the mid-fifties, Clifford Hall, a funeral director from LaFayette, was the duly appointed Indian Agent. Mr. Hall was very helpful and informative in Indian affairs. I called upon him many times for assistance in sensitive investigations.

The relationship that I had with the reservation was founded on many hours of dedicated effort. During my tenure in the LaFayette area, which spanned eighteen years, I became very familiar with all the families on the reserve. The people from the reserve that I had contact with were very intelligent and possessed a great sense of humor. I am certain that there were a few who didn't like to see a troop car coming down the road, but they were in the minority. I took the time to understand their culture, which resulted in mutual respect for each other. I remember well some of the flack that I used to get from my co-workers because of my dedication to the Indian people. Often I heard, "He's baby-sitting the Indians." Again another example of organizational dynamics.

I can only say that during those eighteen years I never had to draw my service revolver nor use a baton on any member of the tribe. When I effected an arrest on the reservation it was always accomplished in an orderly manner. It astounds me that some arresting officers had to resort to physical confrontation to make an arrest on the reserve. The words of the late former Superintendent Albin Johnson during my entrance interview with him, echo in my mind: "Trooper Briant, a tough cop isn't one that necessarily uses force, but instead displays good common sense." I have always remembered that definition over the years. Many others apparently never heard it; no wonder there are so many problems in this world.

Maintenance of troop cars is a very important function. It is imperative that the schedule for each vehicle be monitored. LaFayette was no exception. When I first arrived at the barracks there, the most accessible service station was located at the intersection of Routes 11 & 20. The oil and filter would be changed, the vehicle would be greased, and a cursory examination of the fan belts and water hoses would be routine.

Tires on the troop car are especially very important. They have to be constantly checked for wear and proper tread. (How embarrassing it would be for a Trooper to issue a citizen a traffic summons for "unsafe tire" only to have the citizen check the Trooper's car tires and find them worn smooth. Talk about red faces!)

Seriously, a Trooper chasing a speeder at 100 miles per hour must feel confident that his or her tires are in 1st-class condition. In the fifties it wasn't uncommon for a Trooper to pursue a fleeing motorist at high speeds for long periods of time. You might say, "Use your radio." That's easy enough to do; however, usually there would not be another troop car within thirty miles.

The adoption of radar across the State of New York in 1958 was a vital tool for the Troopers to curb excessive speed and, most important, thus save human lives. During that year Troop "D" created its first radar team under the direction of Technical Sergeant Clayton Snook, Supervisor of the Traffic Bureau.

The three selected radar operators attended an in-service school in the Albany area. The first units were manufactured by Automatic Signal Inc. of Norwalk, CT. Each was a transceiver, a rectangular box fastened to a three-legged tripod, with a fifty-foot cord and a hundred-foot cord. Either of these cords would be attached to a graph situated within the troop car, and a visual meter would be attached to the graph. Once the transceiver, the graph, and the visual meter box were connected together, a regular fully charged automobile battery would be attached to another cord going into the transceiver unit, to provide energy.

The radar operator would then be in a position to start the task of tuning the radar with a tuning fork, one set at 40 m.p.h. and one at 60 m.p.h.. After being struck on one's hand or arm, the tuning fork then would be placed in front of the transceiver, thus activating the stylus pen on the graph. When the operator initiated the tone of the 40 m.p.h. tuning fork, this reading was registered as a blip on the paper graph like a scroll. The readings would be noted on the graph along with the date and time of the test and initialed by the operator. Once this was noted on the graph, a pickup troop car with a calibrated speedometer (all troop cars used in traffic enforcement are calibrated once or twice a year) would pass the unit. When the troop car passed the transceiver at 40 m.p.h., the stylus pen and visual meter would again be activated, and another forty m.p.h. blip would be displayed on the graph paper. The operator would initial this blip with the date and time. This procedure was followed each time the radar was set up for traffic enforcement; at the beginning of the detail and at the conclusion of the detail, with all required endorsements. The graph would be used for court purposes in the event of a trial. It was always handled as potential evidence, under the control of the radar operator.

When the radar unit is used, it is most important that the speed zone be a legal one. Speed zones in New York were established, erected and maintained under the direction of the New York State Traffic Commission. One time in 1959, when the radar was set up properly and in operation, we apprehended a highway superintendent from a northern New York State county. He contested the summons and pled not guilty. His contention in court was the fact that the speed zone in which we were operating the radar was not legal. His contention was correct, and the case was dismissed. He argued that the particular speed zone did not have an adequate warning sign displayed as he entered the speed zone. The warning sign had been apparently removed by vandals. A new sign was erected.

I should mention that the radar operates on the Doppler shift theory; the difference between the transmitted and the received frequency determines the speed. The unit always operated in favor of the motorist. That is, if the battery source weakened, the readings on the visual meter and graph would be less than the actual speed the target car was travelling.

Each operator would have the radar unit in his area for a ten-day period. At the end of the tenth day, the operator would make the proper arrangements to turn the unit over to the next operator. I was assigned to the radar detail for ten days a month for a two-year period. Working with the radar was a learning experience which went beyond those days on duty with it, however I was also required to attend civic functions in my district relative to the subject of "Radar Use in Traffic Enforcement of Excessive Speed."

When not engaged in the ten-days-a-month radar detail, I assumed my regular duties.

The work continued at LaFayette. The new construction of Route 81 north and south lanes through the LaFayette patrol area signified the changing of times and trends for the area. It increased activity; however, it did not increase staff personnel at LaFayette before 1960.

Corporal McDermott, promoted to Sergeant, was transferred out of the barracks. When Bill left, Trooper Stanley Kogut became Station Commander. A little later, Trooper Neil Belmont transferred to another station. We did maintain the four uniform troopers. Cpl. James Cerino was also promoted, and BCI duties were taken over for the district by Zone Headquarters.

The new highway construction increased our criminal mischief complaints. Road machinery was damaged. Barriers were stolen and tipped over. The detour near Nedrow became a curse, with its uphill curve to the right for southbound traffic, on which many, many semi-trailers would break their axles, thus backing up traffic. It was an everlasting nightmare for the Troopers at LaFayette until Route 81 was officially opened.

Continuous duty of 120 hours a week kept playing havoc with my married life. My job became my number one priority.

During the first part of 1957, Peggy told me the good news: she was pregnant. She stayed on for another six months with the New York Telephone Company. The three months before the birth was a time of patience and great care. She didn't want another miscarriage. I helped her as much as I could.

The early evening of October 1st, 1957, was an exciting time for both of us—I guess I could say the three of us. John Edward was delivered by Dr. James Coville at the Syracuse Memorial Hospital. When I was allowed to see him, my heart raced with joy and happiness. A handsome "wee" lad was he. After I left the hospital, I purchased a large box of the best cigars I could find. Peggy was a mom and I was a daddy.

We had arranged a small nursery in the apartment on Ford Avenue. Five days later little John Edward was in his new home. Peggy was weak, but made a quick comeback. Julia came to visit and assist with the newborn. I went back to work.

Thank God for Julia Brennan, Peggy's mother! I could return to duty and not have to worry about changing the diapers on John Edward for those first two weeks until Peggy got her strength back. John was a good baby and slept most of the night without waking up. He had his dad's blue eyes. He brought a great deal of joy into our home.

All the personnel at the LaFayette barracks congratulated me about my newborn son. I waited to hear the congratulations from each before I handed over the cigar. Words cannot express the pride I held in my heart for John Edward.

It was back to duty and those long days and nights away from home. As members of the New York State Troopers, it was required that our uniforms be kept spotless. The dry cleaning truck stopped by the LaFayette barracks once a week. The driver would hang up the freshly dry cleaned uniforms and picked up the soiled ones. There was nothing like a freshly cleaned uniform to start the day off right. The driver from the cleaning company was a friendly fellow and enjoyed talking with the Troopers. When this service was discontinued after a period of time, we had to drive to the Zone Headquarters once a week to drop off and pick up the uniforms. Fortunately, when Route 81 was completed, going to North Syracuse was not difficult. Prior to that time a Troop car would find itself in heavy traffic congestion in the Village of North Syracuse.

All of us assigned to LaFayette respected all our local Justices of the Peace. These gentlemen would respond at any time of the day or night. Over the years we appeared in their offices with a cross-section of America. Very seldom did we experience any trouble with the defendants who appeared with us. Then, when the handling of violations through the mail was adopted, it relaxed the crowded courts on court night. The local Justices had previously scheduled their court nights prior to the handling of violations through the mail. There were seldom any conflicts with the mail-ins.

Several of the Justices were farmers, and sometimes they had to have their hired men start the milking of the cows because the Judge would be holding court in his office or in the dining room. Some Judges were attorneys, and sometimes we had to call them at their law firms. We had a good working relationship.

The Justices were not the only people with whom we worked. There were the towing people who would respond twenty-four hours a day. These people would come to a scene and pitch right in and help.

The firefighters, the ambulance people, the highway people from the Town, State and County—I haven't the room in this book to list them all. It was all the people, all the time, who made the system work.

In Nedrow, for example, anyone passing by the intersection of Rockwell Road on Route 11 between 8:00 a.m. and 9:30 a.m. would see the faithful crossing guard, Lillian Clark, monitoring the children for the Rockwell Elementary School. Lil's eyes were always on the traffic and the kids. In the afternoon she would be there doing the same thing. We had a wonderful working relationship.

Betty Bigsby, another crossing guard, in the Village of Tully, staffed a busy intersection in the morning and afternoon. Like Lillian, Betty kept a trained eye on the children and did an excellent job for years.

During my eighteen years at LaFayette, Lillian and Betty,

monitored the safety of hundreds of school children, and assisted the writer in many of his cases. They were both outstanding citizens, and their chief concern was the children.

The activity at the LaFayette Station repeated itself over and over: accidents involving cars, trucks, farm machinery, airplanes, railroad trains, motorcycles, and bicycles, as well as the homicides, suicides, hunting accidents, drownings, floods, fires, robberies, and more. Such incidents fill the pages of time, and have an everlasting effect on the Trooper, comparable to action in a military organization during a war time condition. The war, however, usually ends in a few years, while the stress on the police officer can be unbearable as their combat goes on forever. Even after retirement, an officer who was worth his or her salt while on the job still feels the emotional trauma left by some of the vivid memories witnessed on duty. Only in the past few years have police administrators taken a good look at the problem.

When the lease ended, Peggy, Johnny and I moved from the Onondaga Garden Apartments to a larger 3rd floor apartment at 206 West Borden Avenue in Syracuse. In the latter part of 1958, the time of the move, I was attending in-service school in Albany. Peggy and some of our friends moved us to the new address while I was in school. Some of these friends told me later Peggy had loaded all our canned goods into the bottom of a folding couch. The men who lifted the couch couldn't believe it weighed so much. They soon found the cause of the added weight, and unloaded the canned goods, and continued up the three flights of stairs.

A few days later I returned to find the two-bedroom apartment settled in and, of course, immaculate. It seemed to me that in a week's time little John had grown taller. When I arrived at the apartment to join Peggy for supper, he was in his playpen stacking wooden blocks. Peggy told me all about the move and how wonderful our friends had been to give her the assistance. The move could not have been made without them.

During the years prior to 1960, while assigned to LaFayette, we Troopers always tried to attend church services. At the time I belonged to St. Leo's in Tully. I attended church with Corporal McDermott. We knew just about everybody in the congregation.

It was during this time that Corporal McDermott sponsored me for membership into the Cortland Knights of Columbus. I met many people from the Cortland area while a member of the Knights. A well known Masonic member from Fayetteville approached me about joining the Fayetteville Lodge. I thanked him for the consideration, but declined because of my already busy schedule.

Over the years I attended many funerals in LaFayette, Tully, and Syracuse. Most of the people who died were from the LaFayette patrol area. Many were friends who passed away from natural causes or had been accident victims. There was a strong sense of community and when one of the townspeople passed on, the loss was felt by all. Some of the closeness of the community was prompted by events sponsored by various churches and clubs; they put on chicken dinners, turkey dinners, spaghetti dinners, and ham-and-cabbage boiled dinners. I made it a point to attend these functions. I always maintained high visibility in the district because it offered good communication with all the citizens. The dinners occurred in every township of the LaFayette patrol area. I did not do so for personal recognition. All the citizens of the community have the taxpayer right to law enforcement service, and I made certain, during my tenure, that's what they received.

Of course, in any organization, whether it be law enforcement or industry, there will always be the armchair strategist with clandestine ideologies. I always endeavored to be self-reliant, and during my entire career it was my philosophy to "do it my way", eliminating bureaucracy and red tape. This approach, however, does not offer one much chance for advancement and sets one up for a moving target. It is not my desire to name individuals in this book that enjoyed "taking shots" at me. I simply wish to say that no matter what time period we live in, or which field of endeavor that one chooses to pursue, there will always be the "shooters" and the "targets." They come in all shapes and sizes.

In 1960 Trooper Stanley Kogut, my partner for several years and Station Commander of the LaFayette barracks, decided to leave the Troopers and go into business for himself. I didn't want to see Stan leave. He was a good supervisor, fair and just in his command position. Several of us tried to talk him out of it, but his mind was made up and he terminated his employment.

Shortly after Stanley left, Lieutenant Harry Blaisdell stopped by the LaFayette barracks and gave me the news: Trooper Briant was to become the new Station Commander! The Lieutenant told me the reasons for my new assignment and added that I would be dropped from the radar detail. A teletype message would be forthcoming he said as he wished me good luck. When he left the barracks to return to Zone Headquarters at North Syracuse, the butterflies in my stomach started a ballet dance. I was overjoyed, but somewhat apprehensive.

In April, 1960 my promotion to Station Commander became official. I was one of several Senior Troopers who had the distinction of holding the position of Station Commander throughout Troop D.

I was now officially in charge of the LaFayette Patrol area. This challenge was unexpected; however, I knew deep in my heart that I would do my best to succeed.

Two weeks of annual vacation started on April 12. Peggy, John Edward, and I loaded the car and drove to Massachusetts to be with Julia. We hadn't been able to visit with her very much and thought this would be a good time to make the trip.

Everything seemed to be looking up for us, and then the sad news came. On the evening of April 16th, my mother called me at Julia's and told me of my Father's passing. When I told Mother that I would leave immediately, she asked me not to leave for Auburn until the next morning, fearful for my making the long drive in the dark. I fought to keep the tears back as I hung up the telephone. When I told Peggy and everyone the news of Father's passing, everyone broke down. I was devastated. He had been such a wonderful Father, always struggling for the betterment of his family. A feeling of sorrow and emptiness overwhelmed me. I worried about my Mother. Peggy comforted me. Father had died of a heart attack.

The next day we left Julia's at about 5:00 a.m. for Auburn. It was a quiet ride. Peggy and Johnny knew that I was stricken with grief. Their tears flowed with mine.

Mother met us at the door. My brother and his wife were there, as well as my sister Joan. Uncle Gerald and Aunt Fannie had driven down from Alexandria Bay, New York. Other relatives soon arrived.

The funeral arrangements were made at Kelly's Funeral Home in Weedsport. It had been Father's wishes to be laid to rest in the Weedsport rural cemetery. He had had a special closeness to that community. For ten years father had attended the firemen's field days and during that time made thousands of Aunt Sarah's fried cakes for that gala affair. He would donate his fried cake fryer and expertise at no cost to the department. We honored Father's wishes.

During visiting hours, hundreds of people, some unknown to me, paid their respects to our father whom we loved so very much. Two days later he was laid to rest in the plot by the fence on a small knoll in the Weedsport Rural Cemetery. The rolling green knolls of the cemetery were like waves in the ocean. Father and mother had previously visited this part of the cemetery when they purchased their burial lots, and this was Father's choice location.

We all met at the family home that Father had built. It was a sad time for all of us. Uncle Gerald, my mother's brother, gave a great deal of comfort to us, which will always be remembered.

Peggy, John Edward, and I stayed with Mother a few days to comfort her. Before the rest of the family left for their homes, I thanked my aunt and uncle for their constant assistance and compassion at this sorrowful time in our lives. When Peggy, John Edward, and I left for Syracuse the following day, there was silence and tears and broken hearts.

The grieving period lasted for weeks. I found myself reflecting on happier days with my Dad. I only wished that I could have made a greater effort to have spent more time with him prior to his death.

Mother continued to work at the shoe factory in Auburn. We had asked her to come and live with us, and she had told us that she appreciated our kindness, but chose to stay in her home. We respected her wishes.

Many added duties landed on my shoulders as the new Station Commander of LaFayette. I was responsible for all monthly activity reports—including public assembly, posted property, fuel consumption—as well as station inventory, teletype messages, fuel tank measurements, and everything concerning the proper operation of a State Police patrol station.

In addition, I was responsible for the cleaning of the patrol station. We kept a small fund to purchase bowling alley wax for our station's hardwood floors. All the station personnel, including myself, kept the station immaculate. We buffed the floors every day and applied wax once a week.

We installed the storm windows for the winter season and in the spring removed them and installed screens. We washed the station windows every week. Not only the interior of the station was maintained; we mowed the grass on our hilly lawn with a hand mower.

The Zone Lieutenant, Troop D Officers, and Inspecting Officers always found the LaFayette Barracks well policed and there was very little criticism of the Station operation and activities of the assigned personnel.

It was during 1960 after I had been appointed Station Commander that I noticed the beginning of a change in Division policy. All Station Commanders were required to submit in-depth reports concerning population trends within their assigned districts. The move was on to reduce the work week of Trooper's from 120 hours to 60 hours. With the change, a Trooper would work 12 hour shifts for a total of five work days each week. This change would add new Troopers to the Division of State Police. It would also permit the Trooper to have a more normal life-style, allowing the Trooper to go to his home at the end of his duty shift. Such changes would enlarge the State Police force and would mean new promotions. It would also do away with barracks life as we knew it.

The changes came rapidly. These new modifications were being directed by our new Superintendent, Arthur Cornelius, formerly of the Federal Bureau of Investigation and the banking industry. The new Superintendent restructured the Division of State Police and modernized it.

On the LaFayette Station level, the change brought about a new training schedule for novice Troopers. Many Senior Troopers became Trooper trainers. I was selected to add Trooper training to my duties as Station Commander.

During 1960, 1961, 1962 and part of 1963 I was assigned new rookies, one at a time. The new rookie would be under my control and direction for one to two months. I was privileged; all the individuals assigned to me went on to be quite successful in their State Police careers. I had to submit reports on each member on a timely basis, denoting the progress and making recommendations necessary. I trained ten to thirteen people during this additional assignment.

I found training to be a learning experience, not only for the rookie, but for myself. Each of the high-quality recruits possessed the proper fiber to become a State Trooper. Even if they hadn't had it, they were given plenty of opportunity to achieve their goal by a great deal of hard work. My experience with the recruit training program showed it to be very rewarding.

In July 1963 I was summoned, along with the Station Commanders of Dewitt and Elbridge, to Zone Headquarters for a Station Commanders' meeting. There we became acquainted with our new Zone Lieutenant, Donald W. Ambler. He was a tall, lean man with red hair and a pleasant personality. He had been a U.S. Marine prior to entering the State police.

He struck me as the type of leader a person would follow into a burning building. I knew right away that I was dealing with a true professional. Lieutenant Ambler outlined his Zone policies, and told us that he expected full compliance. Before the meeting concluded, he informed us that his door is always open and that if we had any doubts about important decisions that might come up in running a station we should call him or stop by. As I stood up at the meeting's end, the Lieutenant turned to me.

"John, before you leave, would you come into my office?"

"Yes, sir." I replied. I was puzzled.

I entered the office and approached his desk.

He continued, in an authoritative tone. "John, I have a letter from the Troop Commander relative to a complaint a citizen has made against the LaFayette Station. It concerns the handling of Juvenile cases. This citizen alleges that there have been several incidents involving youths under the age of sixteen and there has been no criminal action taken against them. I want you to conduct an investigation and submit your findings to me in a period of ten days—the irate citizen is one, Joseph Smith."

"Yes, sir." I replied. I saluted the Lieutenant. I was perplexed as I left the office.

On the return trip to the LaFayette Station I tried to remember all the Juvenile cases that had come to our attention. I also thought about the irate citizen, Joseph Smith. I had heard of this person before—as a trouble maker.

During the next ten days, another Trooper and I spent most of our time looking up the cases that involved children under the age of sixteen. The cases involved burglary of a resident where alcohol had been taken, several criminal-mischief complaints, and a stolen-car case. We made a list of the complainants and re-interviewed each one; as in the first instance, each maintained a firm stance of no criminal action against the Juvenile(s) involved, and all of them indicated that they would submit to sworn statements on behalf of the New York State Police to that effect.

Within a ten-day period, the required investigative report was on the desk of Lieutenant Ambler, who forwarded it along with his report, to Troop Headquarters for further action. On July 26, Captain J.C. Miller submitted all case papers to Division Headquarters attn: Superintendent Arthur Cornelius for his information and guidance.

The matter was closed. The complaint against the LaFayette Station and the handling of Juvenile matters was unfounded. The complainant was notified by the Troop Commander as to his findings. The investigation did uncover the fact that the complainant did have a record for Vehicle and Traffic Law violations. A long record.

In my heart I knew that all Juvenile cases had been handled properly. The re-interviews conducted only added to our workload. However, I was elated to inform the members of our barracks that we were exonerated. This was another example of the "shooters" and the "targets."

The LaFayette patrol had it moments of excitement. Two major highways ran through our district during the 1960's. They were Route U.S. 11 and Route U.S. 20. A third major highway in the process of being built was Route 81. An incident occurred near the Hamlet of Nedrow on Route U.S. Route 11 at about 11:00 p.m. on one winter's night. A snow storm was in progress.

Clifford Hayden, age 42, of South Onondaga, was to meet me in Nedrow to discuss lighting and reflector equipment for several new trucks his company had purchased. I was waiting in my patrol car in the parking lot of the Webster's Dairy Bar. Mr. Hayden pulled his car into the lot and joined me. We had started to discuss the New York State Law concerning the required lights and reflectors, when I noticed in my rearview mirror that a Ford Station Wagon having the same description of a wanted stolen car from the Auburn area was traveling southbound on Route 11.

I quickly told Mr. Hayden that two men had escaped from the new Cayuga County Jail, and that they were believed to be in a car just like the one that had just passed, which was wanted in a fifteen-State alarm. I informed Hayden that I was pressing him into service to check out the vehicle in question.

We rapidly overtook the Ford Station wagon. As we approached from the rear, our headlights showed only one occupant. We called a

Signal 30 to the North Syracuse Zone Headquarters and Troop D Headquarters. The response was that the car and occupants were wanted and to use caution in the apprehension.

With the red light flashing and the siren blaring, we attempted to pull the station wagon over. They wouldn't budge. I told Hayden to take my shotgun and insert one shell into the chamber, but to leave the safety on.

The car finally edged to the side of Route 11 and stopped. One subject got out of the car from behind the steering wheel. I could see that the second subject was lying on the floor in the rear of the station wagon. I told him to get out of the car with his hands up. We did not know whether they had weapons, and we were ready for anything. The subject in the rear of the car got out and shouted loudly, "I have nothing to live for except the road gang of the Virginia Correctional system!"

We didn't know whether the escapees would attack or run, but when Hayden pulled the hammer back on the shotgun I knew that we were in charge. The escapees became very quiet. Both of the men were wearing coveralls with pockets containing several heavy tools, which could have been used to assault Hayden and me. We didn't give them the chance to bash our heads in. With Hayden holding the cocked single shot shotgun and me showing my drawn revolver, we steered them to the rear door of my troop car.

Hayden held the shotgun on them as I removed the tools from their long, deep coverall pockets. I cuffed both men securely and ushered them into the rear seat of the troop car. My police car radio was blaring. Zone headquarters was trying to reach me. I grabbed the radio mike and proudly notified headquarters that the apprehension was successful and the jail escapees were secured. They were identified as William Bassett, age 20, of Petersburg, VA, and Roger B. Stiney, age 24, of New York City.

We looked to the south and saw a long string of red lights and heard sirens blaring. I would say there were fifteen police cars from three different agencies coming toward us. When they arrived, a Sergeant from the Syracuse Police Department approached me and asked if they could be of assistance. Zone headquarters had notified other police agencies in the area to proceed to the scene to render aid to us. Fortunately we didn't need assistance, however, Hayden and I were glad to see them. We thanked them.

The police cars turned around and proceeded to their respective jurisdictions. Hayden and I, with a feeling of triumph, and with the apprehended escapees, sped off to zone headquarters. On our arrival we were met by the Troop Commander, who congratulated us. The fifteen-state alarm was canceled.

I submitted a memo to my superiors requesting that Mr. Clifford Hayden be awarded a commendation for his unselfish assistance in the apprehension of two jail escapees who were well into their flight from the Central New York area. To this day Mr. Hayden tells his friends how he became a Trooper for a few hours. I can only say that a serious incident could have erupted if Hayden had not been there to assist me on that cold winter's night many years ago.

A few weeks after the apprehension, when I was testifying before a Cayuga County Grand Jury in Auburn, I was told by several members of the Jury that the escapees had walked by my mother's hedge during their escape. I marveled to myself, "What a small world!"

Peggy, John Edward, and I made another move. The neighborhood on West Borden Avenue in Syracuse was beginning to deteriorate, and for the safety of my family I felt that it was time to move.

We found a small home on Barnes Avenue in Syracuse, in the Lady of Lourdes Parish. The house was equipped with gas heat. In researching the previous owner's electric and gas bills I learned that the home would be economical and fit our budget.

For this move I was there to do my share of the lifting and the tugging. The new home was quaint, in a nice, lower middle class neighborhood with a cross-section of the Syracuse work force. A Syracuse Police Officer lived down the street and a City Fireman across the street from us. It was called "Civil Service Row."

We planted shrubs in front of the house and a blue spruce tree in front of the shrubs. The shrubs bordered our front sidewalk. The fenced-in backyard offered a good playground for Johnny. We purchased a swing set and built a sandbox. A small stream ran behind the house, on the other side of the fence.

In the fall of 1961 Peggy again became pregnant. She continued to work with the telephone company until the seventh month of her pregnancy. We arranged one of the small bedrooms into a nursery and decorated it with blue wallpaper, in anticipation that the new arrival would be another son. If not, I would have another wallpapering detail. We didn't care whether it was a girl or boy, as long as our newborn was healthy.

The work at State Police LaFayette during that time was routine: accidents, assault complaints, domestic matters, and talks to schools on highway safety and the duties of the State Police.

Winter was busy with large trucks and buses sliding off the narrow highways. Route 81 through our district was very busy, especially in the mornings before the sand trucks from the Department of Transportation defeated the icy conditions.

The Trooper Recruit Training Program was progressing. Most of the recruits I was privileged to work with came from the western part of New York State. They were true gentlemen and eager to learn. The concept of training with a senior Trooper included the hope that the recruit would adopt some of the older Trooper's good points and then eventually form his own way of doing things, within the parameters of the policy of the Division of State Police.

I certainly did not profess to be the perfect teacher or instructor. I did, however, attempt to instill in these young men the spirit of "common sense" and the work ethic. Although the old saying "You be good to the job and the job will be good to you," doesn't necessarily come true to all people all the time, in my own case, at this time in my life, I was thoroughly dedicated to the New York State Police. Many upper-level supervisors were aware of my dedication and ambition to achieve in the State Police service. It wasn't my makeup to sit idle. I had to keep myself busy in order to be happy. As I look back now I realize I probably gave the impression to many of my co-workers that I was trying to outperform them, but this was not the case at all. My drive probably first showed many years earlier when I worked in the Throopsville Cemetery trimming the grass around the headstones. I probably trimmed more grass than anyone else. This approach to life must be in my genes; my parents were hard-working people.

James Dennis Briant weighed in at under five pounds on June 8, 1962. Dr. James Coville of the Syracuse Memorial Hospital attended Peggy. I was in the waiting room when the tall doctor approached me with the news of a newborn son. Jimmy was born prematurely and didn't leave the hospital with Peggy the day I went to bring her home. In fact, Jimmy was in the special-childcare until his weight increased to six pounds and ten ounces. Peggy and I were very proud, and little Johnny was so happy to have a little brother.

I helped Peggy as much as I could. Julia, happy grandmother, stayed for a few weeks to help her with those necessary duties of attending a newborn. Jimmy was given formula as had been Johnny instead of being breastfed, which allowed Peggy a bit of freedom because others could feed him while she also cared for her toddler. Johnny had torn his playpen apart and was working on a tricycle. Everything seemed to be going very well for us: an ideal family in an ideal environment.

Instead of purchasing one box of cigars I purchased two boxes. They were Dutch Masters panatelas. People got cigars whether they smoked or not. It was a special event, and as with Johnny's birth I was so very proud to be a new poppa.

On my four day passes I would take Peggy and the boys throughout my district and introduce them to everyone I knew. In good restaurants Peggy and I would sit at the table with two boys that smiled at everyone. I cannot recall the boys crying or carrying on as some kids do. We made many visits to those places, and they were fine times. A person could realize more value of a dollar those days in the late fifties and early sixties.

As I stated earlier. the adoption of the twelve-hour workday and thus the comfort in sleeping in one's own bed at home was attributed to the efforts of Superintendent Arthur Cornelius. The restructuring of the Division during his tenure boosted morale.

The pay scale was also reevaluated and the uniform Trooper and the Investigator brought home more money in their paychecks. Of course, the Command Officers were included in the raises, too.

All members of the State Police from time to time receive letters of commendation if their duties are performed well. Of course, other letters could complain about their performance. Fortunately, over the years the large majority of letters that I received were favorable. Then there's the old saying, "Yeah, that and fifteen cents will buy you a cup of coffee." I didn't perform my duties especially to receive a complimentary letter, so to speak, but a few really good ones did come my way. I loved the State police and I loved to help people if I could. It was "me," doing it my way; and when I was praised for it besides, so much the better pleasure for me.

One such letter did please me. It was a letter of Commendation from Mr. Edward R. Murphy, Assistant Attorney General, Department of Law, Albany, New York. The letter made clear that the legal instruments, which consisted of the Information, the Deposition, and the Warrant in the matter of --------- Vs. People of the State of New York, Claim Number XXXXX, have no defects. This case is discussed earlier in this book.

One day during the early 1960's, as I was pulling out of the LaFayette Station's driveway, I was hailed down by a motorist, a gentleman from the Hamlet of LaFayette. He reported that he had returned home from work and found a large sow pig in his front yard. He requested that I follow him to his residence on Route 11.

I pulled into his yard behind him. I was amazed at what I saw: a huge sow that must have weighed three hundred pounds! The animal had uprooted the ground around his entire house and practically dug up his septic tank and drain field. I could appreciate the complainant's feeling of being invaded.

I told the complainant that I would investigate the incident and secured all the pertinent information for my report. In the meantime, I placed a telephone call to LeRoy Baker, a local farmer nearby. Mr. Baker and a hired hand soon arrived with their stake-racked truck.

It took some doing, but all of us managed to get the sow headed in the direction of the rear end of the truck and induced her to climb onto a lowered tailgate. I requested of Mr. Baker that he maintain the sow in his barn while I attempted to locate the owner. All of us in the yard had an idea who owned the sow, a pig farmer from Cardiff. This was not the first time one of his pigs had gotten out of the pen. This particular sow had wandered a long distance from the owner's farm. Mr. Baker assured me that he would secure it in his barn. I advised our complainant to contact his insurance company.

When I pulled into the pig farmer's driveway, he was just entering his barn. I got out of the Troop car and went over to him. I told him that one of his sows had apparently gotten loose from the pen, and I described the damage caused at our complainant's residence. The farmer said, "That sow isn't one of mine." Knowing that it would be futile to argue with him, I left. The whole town soon heard about the incident, and it was everyone's belief that the pig farmer denied ownership because he did not want to pay for the damages the sow had caused.

About two weeks later the telephone rang at the LaFayette barracks one morning. It was Leroy Baker calling. He seemed excited and asked me to come to his farm immediately.

When I arrived at the Baker farm I soon learned why he was so excited. The sow had given birth to nine little piggies! Mr. Baker told me that he had named the sow "Jacquie" and that he would care for "Jacquie" for as long as the State Troopers requested. I informed him that in sixty days if the owner were not located or did not come forth to claim the sow and the piggies, they would be auctioned off at the local auction barn in Apulia Station. I further advised him that the money received from the sale would be his to compensate for the care and upkeep of the sow and her little ones. Mr. Baker had come to the aid of Troopers over the years, and was a good citizen and neighbor to the community.

United Press International ran the story of the sow and her newborn, and letters from all over the country poured into the State Troopers' mailbox at the post office. A radio station called from the Midwest and inquired as to how "Jacquie" and her piggies were doing.

The owner of "Jacquie" never came forward to claim her and the offspring. In a couple of months "Jacquie" and the piggies were auctioned off. Mr. Baker was compensated.

At the time, "Jacquie" became a household word in the LaFayette patrol district. The complainant's insurance company came to his rescue, and I sent a letter to Mr. LeRoy Baker, thanking him for his assistance in this case.

During my tenure at the LaFayette Station, the citizens of that community and the other communities within our district, including the Onondaga Indian Nation, gave us one hundred percent cooperation, one hundred percent of the time. It was indeed a privilege for me to devote eighteen years of my life to the community. To this day, almost forty-one years since my assignment to LaFayette, I still receive letters from many of the families in the district. The spirit of their Citizen/Trooper cooperation will be forever in my memory.

My firm belief in the State Troopers, and my years of unwavering dedication to serve above and beyond the required duty, also did cause me a great deal of heartache and hardship.

TPR George Loomis out-side SP Pulaski, Troop D, 1954.

Those Were The Days...

. . .when in 1954 the late Sgt. Larry Fox joined his SP Waterloo troopers for a group shot as icicles hung from the station roof. From left are Tpr. R. F. Boyle (Canandaigua traffic), Tpr. J. F. Schuyler (Oneida), Inv. J. H. Briant (Lafayette), retired Sr. Inv. C. P. Cox, an unidentified trooper, and Z/Sgt. A. J. Quinn (Liverpool). Photo courtesy of Inv. Briant.

from The Trooper magazine.

Trooper John H. Briant from the LaFayette Barracks at The Onondaga Indian Nation, 1958.

Briant and partner with members of the Nedrow Volunteer Fire Department south of Nedrow at the scene of a truck accident. Late '60s.

Trooper John Briant, Station Commander, SP LaFayette, 1960's.

John and sons James and John in The North Country, 1964.

Investigator J.H. Briant and Detective Maurice Touhey, OCSD with armed shooter, subdued five minutes after this UPI photo. The man at this time was still armed with a loaded and cocked .32 cal. revolver under his T shirt.

Superintendent William Kirwan presents The Brummer Award for Bravery to Investigator John Briant in Albany, February 4, 1971.

John and brother David in Glendale, Arizona in the 1980's.

John and Marge renews acquaintance with Roy Clark in Branson, MO.

John and Crackers, 1980's.

John and Marge on a trip to New Hampshire, 1986.

In 1964 I divorced my wife Peggy. John and Jimmy stayed with their mother in the home I turned over to her. It was like suffering a death. The pain has been everlasting. I am certain that they suffered as I have. At the time all I had was my job. Anyone who is divorced soon finds out who their true friends are. The letters from friends and family become less frequent. The co-workers chatter among themselves and as you pass them in a hallway to your office, they become silent. During the two years after the divorce, I visited my sons as often as I could. At the end of this two-year period Peggy, remarried—a fine gentleman from Massachusetts—and sold the house in Syracuse. The two boys, nine and four years of age, moved with their mother, and it became extremely difficult to arrange visitation to see them. The divorce agreement left me without sufficient funds to travel there. I did see my sons occasionally over the years. I am sure to this day they have never forgiven me.

Eventually, I remarried. Mary, a widow had one son. We moved to Port Byron and rented a half a house. Her son entered Port Byron School and graduated. He was an athlete. After graduation her son joined the United States Air Force. Mary worked at the Port Byron Central School as a teacher's aid, until we moved to another rental property in Liverpool.

In 1963 the LaFayette Station was closed due to budgetary cutbacks, as were the Elbridge and Dewitt Stations. The personnel from the three stations went to the New York State Fairgrounds. There was no change in personnel, and we maintained the same work schedules. We worked out of the fairgrounds for several months until the new Liverpool Station on Beechwood Avenue became operational.

The new barracks, leased for a period of time, was an "L" shaped cement block building. The front desk was located by the front door. There were uniform Sergeants' offices and offices for Bureau of Criminal Investigation personnel. A large room held stand-up metal lockers for each assigned member. The building was quite crowded with all of the uniform Troopers and BCI people assigned there.

I still kept my status as the Senior Trooper for the LaFayette district and I still maintained my contacts, informants and dedication to the people of the southern part of Onondaga County. Often it was rather difficult getting to our assigned areas because of heavy traffic or weather conditions. That period was a busy time for all of us, and a trying time, too.

One cold day in 1965, Mary and I were at our home in Port Byron New York. The telephone rang. An officer from Troop D Headquarters at Oneida informed me that I was being promoted to the Bureau of Criminal Investigation. He told me I would be assigned a car and I would be operating out of the Liverpool Station.

Surprised and needing time to think, I asked the officer if I could call him back after I conferred with my wife. He told me that it was alright to call him back. I thanked him and hung up the telephone.

Mary and I talked about the offer for over an hour. I told her that I felt very honored, but I didn't feel that I could accept the promotion. I told her I didn't have funds to attire myself as a member of the bureau. I also indicated that I enjoyed my duties in the LaFayette district. After our discussion I called the officer back and told him I was declining. I didn't give any specific reason, except that I enjoyed my present duty assignment. I could tell that the officer was disappointed in my decision to not accept the promotion. It was a difficult choice for me to make. I was still carrying a great deal of heartache over my divorce. I felt that I couldn't give my best to the BCI at this time in my life. The work responsibilities in the bureau were different than uniform duties. In the BCI my work would entail the in-depth investigation of criminal acts against society involving numerous crimes of a serious nature. Many of these investigations might take me to other jurisdictions to follow up on leads. At the time I didn't feel I was up to this transition. My dedication was aimed at serving the LaFayette district. I had put a great deal of time and effort into my present assignment, and preferred to stay there.

Many notable people had passed through the LaFayette Patrol district during my tenure of 1955 to 1973. One particular gentleman resided on the Onondaga Indian Reservation. In his youth, Chief Big Tree (Isaac Johnny John) had been considered "the best bare-back rider" and appeared in such films as *Drums Along The Mohawk*, *Unconquered*, *Western Union*, *Stagecoach*, *Last of The Mohicans*, *Hudson Bay*, and *Las Vegas Nights*. The Chief's favorite film was *Life of Buffalo Bill*. He had appeared in over one hundred movies, but his best known role was as model for the face of a coin. As a Seneca Chief, his profile was known to millions on the face of the Indian Head nickel. Chief Big Tree was one of three models chosen in 1912 by the artist who designed the coin.

I met the Chief in the mid-sixties, an old man, when his wife reported a burglary of their home. The Chief was bedridden at the time. Stolen in the burglary were some of the Chief's original nickels. The Chief's age was estimated to be anywhere between 90 to 102 years. He himself said he was 102 years old. He was one of the finest gentleman that I have ever had the privilege to meet. Although he was at such an advanced age when I met him, he displayed a great deal of wisdom and revealed a very sharp mind. Two youths were apprehended for the burglary, however the coins were not recovered.

During the mid-sixties I had the honor of escorting Joseph Martin and Douglas Sefton, Special Feature Writers for the New York Daily News, on a tour of the Onondaga Indian Reservation. They were doing a special feature on the New York State Police, covering the relationship between the Indian population and the Division.

We spent the whole day of September 22,1964, on the reservation. I will always remember Joseph Martin and Douglas Sefton for the true professionalism they displayed through their interviewing techniques and their follow-up feature story. I introduced them to many residents of the Reservation including Chiefs, Clan mothers, school officials and many of the wonderful Indian children during the school session. A picture of Indian children and Trooper Briant appeared in the New York Daily News on November 18th. One of the Indian youths told Mr. Martin and Mr. Sefton that he wanted to be a Trooper someday.

Later on I received a commendation from Major Robert Sweeney, of Division Headquarters, for my participation in the Martin and Sefton visit to the Onondaga Indian Reservation. It was a memorable event in my career. The feature story was well done.

During my tenure at the LaFayette barracks our personnel investigated about twelve airplane accidents. Contrary to public opinion, more airplane accidents occur than people would think.

A 23-year-old Marine Corp reservist flying to his home in the State of Maine experienced engine trouble, struck a powerline, and plowed into a pasture lot. He had purchased the plane in the midwest and was headed for Maine at the time of the crash. He sustained head and back injuries. Trooper Francis West assisted me in this investigation.

A pediatrician from Syracuse crashed a single engine Cessna airplane into a house in Nedrow one afternoon. The doctor was one fortunate gentleman not to have been injured in this crash. The house sustained damage to the upper story. The lone occupant in the home was not injured, but was more than surprised to see the airplane on her property. BCI Corporal James Cerino assisted me with this investigation, as well as civil authorities.

A military jet trainer crashed into Skaneateles Lake killing the pilot. This was a tragic death. A young life snuffed out in a moment in time. Several Troopers took part in this investigation, along with military investigators and civil authorities.

On a cold, wet February evening in 1963 I had signed out of service at a Tully restaurant and was in the middle of my supper when I was told by the manager that I was wanted on the telephone.

To my surprise it was Captain Harold T. Muller, Troop Commander of Troop D in Oneida. Captain Muller informed me that two subjects had robbed a couple in their home located in Wilkes-Barre, Pennsylvania. The subjects had fled from Pennsylvania and were headed north toward Syracuse in an old black Buick sedan. The Captain wanted a road block set up at Nedrow immediately. I told the Captain I was en route.

I left the restaurant and headed north on Route 11, stopping at the barracks to pick up a .30-.30 rifle. When I reached Nedrow I met Troopers C.C. Rich and F. Carroll. They climbed into my car and we pulled next to a closed beer joint and shut off our lights. It was a rainy evening, but a streetlight in front of us gave a clear view of the two-laned Route 11.

Within fifteen minutes a black older model Buick flashed by our observation point. We sped after it and pulled it over after a short run. The car contained three people: a male and a female in the front seat and a male in the rear seat. The males were identified as John L. Mangan and Kenneth M. Carlin, both forty years of age. The female was Louella Mangan, wife of John, who was driving the car. Carlin was from Scranton, Pennsylvania, and the Mangans were from Liverpool, New York.

There were no weapons found in their possession. The pockets of the males contained assorted watches and rings containing a total of 30 karats of diamonds and other assorted jewelry, having an approximate total value of $30,000. The wife of Mangan was not charged, and the apprehended fugitives waived extradition, and were turned over to the

Pennsylvania State Police Detectives, along with the recovered jewelry.

The robbers had entered the home of a wealthy Wilkes-Barre couple while they were out and waited for the couple to return. Holding them at knife point, the men had gagged and tied the couple up in their bedroom and burglarized the home of the jewelry that was recovered in this apprehension of two very dangerous felons, who both had extensive criminal records in Pennsylvania and New York.

All three of us involved in the apprehension received commendations from our Troop Commander. I was selected to appear in the Mayor's office of Wilkes-Barre to receive, on behalf of us three, Commendations from Mayor Francis Slattery.

This case was an example of two State Police enforcement agencies working together to bring criminals to justice.

Winter presented an interesting time for the State Troopers because of the hilly and curvy terrain in the southern part of Onondaga County.

Fifty-three children and an alert school bus driver escaped serious injury and possibly death as a Tully School bus careened down a forty-foot embankment during the early morning of March 30, 1961. The driver lost control in deep slush as he rounded a right-hand curve on Route 80 between Vesper and Tully. As the bus made the descent into the gully, it missed six good-sized trees. Six of the children were shaken up, but there were no serious injuries. I credited Dana Houck for his skill in preventing a more serious mishap and possibly the loss of his life and those of his students riding on the bus. It was a lucky day for all concerned.

In February 1963, in the vicinity of the same curve, a tragic accident occurred when an eastbound car from Rochester lost control and struck a westbound car head-on, killing its operator. The deceased, a well-known former jockey who had won the 1915 Preakness riding the filly "Rhine Maiden," was Douglas Hoffman of Neuman Road, Tully. Douglas was an outstanding citizen of the community and a good friend to all of us. For me and the Troopers who assisted me, it was a difficult accident to investigate. The operator of the eastbound car was arrested for failing to keep right.

During my tenure in the LaFayette district, many fine people involved in mishaps were seriously injured and killed. In those years the New York State Troopers were called on to investigate the majority of the accidents and complaints. I always felt that the reason for this constant activity was the fact that we were so visible to the citizens of the various communities. In addition, I had made it my business to go forth and continually remind the citizens that the Troopers were there to help in any emergency. It was not necessary to post power poles and telephone booths with advertisements of State Police presence, in those years. We were out there and the public knew it.

The reader should bear in mind that a police officer is only as good as the public he serves. In the LaFayette patrol area from 1955 to 1973 I lived that concept—not a good will campaign nor a popularity contest, but in fact a lot of hard work to maintain the high quality of police service to the public.

A day didn't go by that I didn't think about my two sons, John and Jimmy. It was very difficult for me not to be with them, not to see them when I wanted to. I knew that Peggy would take good care of them. I didn't know their stepfather; however, I believed that he was a good man. Of course, our old neighborhood was tending my business better than I did. The usual gossip when a divorce takes place. During the fall of 1964 it surprised me to see all those "pious" individuals hanging me in effigy. They had professed their friendship to me prior to the divorce.

The slander wasn't only in the community at large. It was whispered through the halls and offices of my workplace. It showed up in my mail folder at the barracks: articles, notes, and unsigned scraps of paper targeting my sensitivity. This conduct wasn't newly invented; there have been many books written on the subject of organizational behavior. I soon developed a thick skin and considered the immaturity of the attacker, and just worked harder than ever. Actually I adopted the attitude that work was my hobby, and I thoroughly enjoyed it.

The blizzard of 1966 arrived abruptly and soon the highways in Central New York became plugged with snow. I couldn't get to work for two days. Several of the Troopers were stuck in the Liverpool barracks. It took several days to clear the snow and resume normal patrol duties. The public seemed to come to each other's rescue in an attempt to resume normal activity.

There was always a hustle and bustle of activity in and outside of the Liverpool barracks. The uniform staff and the B.C.I. were involved in many cases. Time passed rapidly.

After approximately three years of renting various houses, Mary and I went to look at mobile homes on one pass day and ended up buying one. It was sixty-seven feet in length and twelve feet wide, and I believe we paid about $6,700.00 for it. We located a mobile park on the Apulia Road near LaFayette, and placed the mobile home there. We moved in within a week. The home was cozy, and served the purpose, and matched our dual income.

We lived in the park until 1973. During those years we were privileged to be not far from the hills of Fabius, and enjoyed hunting deer and rabbit. Neither one of us had much nimrod in our genes. The beauty of the area became the hunted, and we captured many glorious scenes through the shutters of our cameras.

Mary's son, Donald, was doing well in the U.S. Air Force and after basic training at Lackland Air Force Base in Texas he entered a mechanical school at the Amarillo Air Force Base in northern Texas. He seemed to enjoy the Air Force, especially after his basic training. When the school was completed, he was assigned to McGuire Air Force Base in New Jersey as a mechanic assigned to the huge C-130 transports.

On December 14, 1967, State Trooper William G. Doyle, age 28, of Pulaski, was shot and killed shortly before 10:00 a.m., when he stopped a stolen car on Route 84 near Parish. It was a tragic loss to his family as well as to the New York State Police. Doyle had been a Trooper for three and a half years when he was shot. He was an outstanding person, and appeared to be a devoted husband, and a credit to the State Police.

The killers had fled the scene, so a massive manhunt was initiated. All barns, buildings, houses and cars in the area were searched. The conclusion of the case came when one of the killers was located on the second floor of a barn. He had shot the other, and gave up without resisting arrest. I participated in the manhunt, and this senseless killing of Trooper Doyle will remain vividly in my memory forever. He was a wonderful young man.

Regardless of petty differences law enforcement officers may encounter with one another, no one should ever underestimate the brotherhood and sisterhood that exists between them. The network of law enforcement officers across our nation is one family that people in our society will have to reckon with if they choose to behave in a deviant way.

Nineteen sixty-eight brought another tragedy to Onondaga

County. Two teenage girls visited a firemen's field day in Mattydale. They left and were last seen walking toward the Village of North Syracuse. The next day a fisherman found them dead in a field off Oxbow Road near Bridgeport.

An extensive investigation was begun. The Onondaga County Medical Examiner's office ascertained that both of them had been murdered. Hundreds of people were interviewed by uniform and B.C.I. members of the State Police. The families of the murder victims were stunned and continue that way today, almost thirty years later. The case remains active. Many uniform Troopers worked on the case in the beginning. They maintained check points in an attempt to ferret out information, to no avail.

I was in uniform at the time and was assigned to assist Assistant District Attorney Leo Hayes. Together we followed many leads in the area of the crime scene. We interviewed many people and secured sworn statements from them. The case today is still active and very much on the mind of the assigned Investigator presently in charge of it. I was assigned to this case for many years and conducted hundreds of lead investigations until my retirement.

The double-homicide investigation assigned to me prompted many lead investigations. One such lead took me to Prince Albert, Saskatchewan in the early 1980's. Information had been developed that a white male, suspected of murdering a California resident, and who fled that State with the victim's car had been arrested in Canada for the attempted murder of two young Canadian females. The suspect was found guilty of the two counts, and was sentenced to 8 to 15 years in the Prince Albert prison. The State of California filed a murder warrant against their suspect. Our investigation reflected that this same person had stayed in a motel in 1968, about twenty miles from where the two victims were found in the double-homicide case.

On my arrival in Prince Albert, I was met by a plainclothes Royal Canadian Mounted Policeman. He was a friendly chap, and told me that during my visit to Prince Albert he would be glad to assist me. I thanked him. I then proceeded to the local car rental agency and picked up my reserved rental car.

During the week that followed I interviewed the suspect and finally concluded that he had nothing to do with our case. We learned that our suspect was in a New York State jail before and after the day the double-homicide occurred.

The Superintendent of the prison advised me that I had been the only New York State Trooper to ever visit his institution. He told me that he understood that New York Troopers were good marksmen with a firearm. He asked me to join him on his private range, so I accepted the challenge.

He furnished me with a three inch Smith & Wesson revolver, and the contest begun. We both fired practice shots and then the official "shoot" began. It was a draw. Both of us had a final score of 272 out of 300. I did inform the Superintendent that we have some experts, who can really shoot, back in the States. We parted friends.

The flight home from Prince Albert via Toronto, Buffalo and Rochester was rough with all kinds of turbulence. My nerves were on edge when I deplaned in Syracuse.

As I previously indicated the double-homicide case is still actively being pursued by the presently assigned BCI Investigator.

In September of 1968, Zone Sergeant Eugene Coletti summoned me into his office. He informed me that I had one more chance to enter the Bureau of Criminal Investigation (BCI). I told the Sergeant that this time I was willing to go into the BCI if called upon. On September 12th, 1968, Trooper J.H. Briant became Investigator J.H. Briant, assigned to the BCI unit at State Police Liverpool. I was subsequently transferred to the State Police barracks in LaFayette in the early 1970's—a beneficial transfer to me, for my array of numerous contacts had become a part of my Trooper life.

IV

New York State Police:
As a Member of The BCI

IV

As a member of the BCI from 1968 to 1970, the case assignments I received at State Police, Liverpool, formed a sound investigative foundation. The BCI unit consisted of approximately seven to twelve members headed by a Senior Investigator. Each investigator was carrying about 250 cases, ranging from homicide to bad checks, and including rape, burglary, arson, robbery, grand larceny, confidential investigations, and indictable misdemeanor cases.

Although I was assigned to the Liverpool BCI Unit, I still maintained my duty assignment over the LaFayette district. When I was on night reserve, I would be assigned cases in other locations within our Station district.

On August 31, 1969, I had just finished interviewing a complainant in the Town of Marcellus in the southern sector of Onondaga County. The complaint concerned a young couple that was renting one of her apartments and apparently using illegal "recreational" drugs and holding drug parties on weekends. On one such weekend it was alleged that a Philippine monkey was roasted alive in the oven of the renters. It was suspected they had also given the monkey some LSD, an unlawful "treat" indulged in by the party-goers. The complainant, wanting the Troopers to know what was going on, reported the incident to us for intelligence purposes.

The complainant and I met on the porch of a gasoline station owner in the area. She did not want the State Police presence at her home because of the nature of the information; she feared the renters might become suspicious. After our conversation, I thanked the lady and started walking toward my BCI car.

As I neared it, I noted that the gasoline station operator was inside the station, so I stopped to thank him for his cooperation.

At that moment a green Pontiac Lemans pulled into the parking area and three young men got out and went into a store. They immediately came back out. Two re-entered the Lemans while the driver came into the gas station, where I was. He asked the owner if he could obtain five dollars on his credit card, as he was broke and was headed to New York City. The owner agreed, opened the cash register, and took out a five-dollar bill. The owner made out the credit card slip and the driver signed it, then said "thank you" to the gas station operator and left.

The transaction appeared to be alright, but my sixth sense directed me to check out the Lemans and its occupants. But as I approached the driver's door, he hurriedly put the car in reverse. The car stalled and his face became crimson red. I identified myself, displaying my shield and I.D. Card, and told him to get out of the car. He complied and nervously asked me what was wrong.

I requested to see his driver's license and registration for the Lemans. He produced the required items. They were both in the name of Donald Smith of Hialeah, Florida. I questioned him further. He told me he liked the police—a strange statement to make, I thought—and indicated that he was a banker on vacation. He said that he had been visiting his sister in Salem, Ohio, and while he was there the police stopped him several times. He went on to explain that he had re-registered the Lemans with the Ohio Registry, which was why he was displaying Ohio plates. He also claimed that he had left the new Ohio registration at his sister's home by mistake.

I requested the alleged Mr. Donald Smith to accompany me to my BCI car for the purpose of obtaining a special file check on his name, the Florida registration number, and the Ohio plate number. He nervously got into the car with me. I informed him that we had to drive to a nearby steep hill for clearer radio reception. He seemed calm, but again my instinct told me that something was wrong with his story.

The subsequent special file check revealed that the Lemans was wanted in connection with the kidnaping of a Florida banker, Donald Smith, and that the occupants of the car were suspected in the crime. Zone headquarters assured me that assistance was en route to my location.

I immediately handcuffed the subject. He admitted that he was Dennis Dale Hunter, age 20, of Salem, Ohio. He went on to say that he had been serving time at the Ohio State Reformatory at Mansfield, and had escaped through an eighteen-inch conduit pipe. two thousand feet in length.

We went back to the stolen car and to my relief the other two subjects were still in the Lemans. The taller of two got out, though, and became first verbally, then physicaly abusive toward me. I quickly subdued him by wrestling him to the ground. The remaining occupant remained silent. Some local farmers had their noses pressed against the window of the gas station, but no one stepped forward to assist me.

Two knives, several credit card slips, and other pieces of evidence were secured from the Lemans. I ordered that a tow truck come to the scene to tow the vehicle to the Liverpool Station. Assistance soon arrived, and we all traveled to State Police, Liverpool, with the prisoners.

Further investigation revealed that the tall man with all the fire and fury was a college student who didn't like the police. He had been hitchhiking to Boston, Massachusetts. After ascertaining that he was not involved in any criminal activity, and giving him a sound scolding, I released him to continue on his way.

The juvenile accompanying Hunter was involved in the kidnaping. The son of a Jordanian diplomat, assigned to the United Nations, he had run away from his home in New York City and was headed to Florida.

The continued investigation revealed Hunter, after making his escape from the Ohio State Reformatory, had headed for Florida. On the way however, he had become involved in a crime spree that involved the thefts of several vehicles, burglaries, and robberies. One such burglary involved an elderly lady who owned a store. She had gone to her attached house after closing to soak her feet in a pan of hot water. While she was soothing her feet, Hunter, who had been observing her in the store, busted in through a window and tied her up. Upon searching her home, he found several paper sacks of money secreted under several pieces of furniture. He took all the money, which totalled approximately twenty-five hundred dollars. Fortunately he had not hurt the woman.

At another residence he had aroused the curiosity of a watchdog and so had climbed a tree. He saw the farmer come out of his house with a rifle or a shotgun. The watchdog stood at the bottom of the tree, barking profusely. The farmer trained a spotlight up the tree, but must have had poor eyesight, for in a little while he took hold of the dog and went back into the house. Hunter had climbed down and stole the farmer's pickup truck.

At another residence he tied up five members of a family and stole their car. Again, fortunately he did not hurt them.

As Hunter had threaded his way to Florida, he had met and "hooked up" with a young Canadian school teacher. He took her to the Bahamas, where he spent all the money with her.

With all his funds exhausted, he had gone to a bus station, where, by chance, he met the diplomat's son. The young man and Hunter decided to steal some money and a car. They waited in the dark near a parked car in a bank parking lot. In an hour or so, a man left the bank and approached his car. This man was, in fact, one Donald Smith, a bank employee who had worked late. Hunter and his accomplice overpowered Smith and sequestered him in the rear seat of his own car.

Hunter got behind the wheel and the trio headed north toward the Georgia border. Hunter foolishly allowed his captive to call his wife from a telephone booth. Smith managed to tell her that he was being kidnaped and that she must contact the authorities as soon as possible.

The car and its occupants crossed over into Georgia about two hours later. Hunter and the juvenile took Smith to a swampy area, tied him to a tree with some ripped toweling, and left him there. But when they came back to steal a ring from his finger, they found out that he had broken free. Hunter and his accomplice hurriedly continued northward.

Near Savannah, they were almost apprehended by the authorities as they entered a Sears and Roebuck store, but managed to elude the police.

Hunter and his accomplice continued north at a high rate of speed. Rounding a curve, they lost control of the Lemans for a short time. They crossed a lawn where a family reunion was taking place and knocked over several tables. Again they outran a sheriff's department patrol. West of Geneva, they decided to pick up the hitchhiker who was headed to Boston.

Hunter and the juvenile were turned over to Federal authorities and returned to Southern Georgia Federal District Court jurisdiction.

While in custody of Federal Marshals, Hunter briefly escaped their custody in Georgia, but was recaptured a short time later. He was sentenced to a Federal Prison in Joliet, Illinois, for a term of twenty-five years.

Sometime during the mid-seventies, Hunter and four others escaped from Joliet. I was assigned to Troop "B", Massena, at the time. Four of the escapees were quickly apprehended, but Hunter entered Canada and abandoned his stolen car with Illinois plates in the Province of Ontario only a few miles from the Massena barracks. Later apprehended by the Canadian authorities near Saskatoon, Sask., he was returned to Joliet.

Several days after the apprehension of Hunter in New York State on August 31, 1969, I received a telephone call from an engineer who worked for the Carrier Corporation in Syracuse. The man refused to give me his name, but went on to tell me that he was Hunter's uncle. He wanted me to know that when Hunter was a five-year-old boy, he was with his mother in a tavern in Salem, Ohio. The man told me the horrifying tale of how Dennis Dale Hunter's mother was shot and killed in front of her young son. I thanked the uncle and told him that Dennis did not appear to be violent.

Because of his family's Diplomatic Immunity, the Jordanian youth was not held accountable for his participation in these events and was returned to his parents.

The citizens of the LaFayette patrol area were pleased as the newly leased State Police Station became functional in the early part of 1970. My official request for transfer to the BCI Unit at LaFayette was honored and became official during that time.

Mary and I purchased a new mobile home, which was located within three miles of the State Police barracks. Mary took a new job with Blue Cross and Blue Shield in Syracuse. The beautiful valley and the surrounding hills gave the area a special sense of nature's captivating aura.

Autumn was our favorite season. The blending colors of the region blanketed the hillsides for miles around. It was equally as beautiful in the winter. Spirals of smoke lazily lifted from the fireplace chimneys scattered throughout the valley. The arrival of spring with the budding of trees and blossoming flowers brought new life to the region. The gurgling streams filled the creekbeds and freshness could be felt. Summer in the valley was comfortable and many cookouts took place, and the aroma of sizzling steaks teased the tastebuds.

The citizens of the LaFayette community and surrounding hamlets and villages were highly pleased that the presence of the Troopers was again in place. It had been such a foolish decision on the part of the State to close the previous barracks. The residents of the southern section of Onondaga County had been angered about the closure. It had been a hardship for the Troopers assigned to LaFayette to work out of the Liverpool Station. For seven years we had plodded our way to the southern section of the county through the City of Syracuse to our patrol area.

I considered myself fortunate to have returned to the area of my choice as a member of the LaFayette BCI unit. My years of contacts with my Indian friends and the community at large were intact. The area was going through a change. The drug culture of the early sixties was growing. Recreational drug use was creeping into the fabric of our society. Many parents contacted our unit concerned about this added social problem. Some parents found pills and marijuana in their homes. To alleviate the trend, locally we went into the schools and gave talks and showed our drug display kits to the students. Among us we emphasized education as one way to combat the drug invasion. But as the drug culture matured, burglaries and robberies increased in our area the same as all across the country.

When a music festival was held in the Watkins Glen area in the seventies, the State Police set up road-check points to monitor drug activity passing through our patrol district en route to it. There were numerous arrests made for Criminal Possession of a Controlled Substance, which resulted in the recovery of bags of marijuana and hashish, as well as an assortment of pills and capsules. Many of the people passing through the district were college kids from the New England states. The majority of these cases were reduced to disorderly conduct. Most of the defendants were released before the arresting officers had even completed their required paperwork. Once again the double standard of our justice system, which I had no control over, failed to mete out the proper punishment to the defendants.

The college kids joked about being arrested and told us that we were just wasting our time. They were informed that the law was specific concerning their possession of the controlled substance. The college kids always seemed to have the last word as they were shuttled to the Town Justice Courts. Their cavalier attitude incensed my code of ethics, as a law enforcement officer and the laws that I was sworn to enforce.

Since those years long gone by, the drug culture has grown and grown and still festers in our society. Cocaine use and heroin use have crept into the upper levels of society, and drug addicts fill all facets of our society with no change in sight. Nowadays, drug-related crimes are a common occurrence.

Education is still imperative in the drug war, shown clearly by all the arrests still being made. Our penal institutions remain filled to capacity as we approach the beginning of the 21st Century.

*   *   *

On July 12, 1970, a Sunday morning, I was on BCI patrol out of the LaFayette barracks. My travels took me to Delphi Falls to meet a confidential informant. In the late forenoon, after my meeting with my informant, I stopped at the Ozark Inn for a bowl of homemade soup.

The Inn was owned and operated by Wayne Schram. Wayne was a former member of a World War II unit known as Darby's Rangers. He was a most capable individual and could handle any situation with common-sense talking or physical persuasion. He had founded the Ozark Mountain Boys, a country western band, and packed the Ozark Inn on weekends for round and square dancing. Wayne and his family were special to me. His nephew, Donald, had worked with my father at the Seneca Ordinance Depot during the early years of World War II.

Donald Schram was a handsome young man, 25 years old in 1943. He had entered the U.S. Army and became a military policeman. His overseas assignment ended only two weeks after his arrival in Italy; he was listed as killed in action, leaving a lovely wife and small child.

Wayne had another nephew, who lived in Weedsport. "Poochy" Schram played football for Weedsport when I was playing for Port Byron. He was real competition on the football field—rough and tough. When you played against "Poochy," anything could happen.

I finished my bowl of chicken noodle soup and said good-bye to

Wayne and his family. My half-hour lunch break was over.

When I got into my BCI car I turned the State Police Radio on, left the parking lot of the Ozark, and headed north toward Route 20. I hadn't gone three miles when I heard Sergeant May calling me on the radio from the North Syracuse barracks. He advised me to proceed to Nedrow.

The Sergeant's voice seemed to have a sense of urgency. I increased my speed and headed west on Route 20. The highway was two-lane and traffic was light.

When I pulled into Nedrow from the south I saw several state police and sheriff cars. It was apparent that something was happening. I pulled into the parking lot of the Nedrow motel.

I got out of the car and was immediately approached by two State Police supervisors. They told me that one Thomas Haley was in possession of a revolver and was threatening suicide. They told me that Haley had hollered out that he would talk only to "Briant."

Troopers and sheriffs were kneeled down holding shotguns as I approached the front of the house. Sheriff's Detective Maurice Touhey was standing outside near the front window of the home owned by Mr. Mark Haley, father of Thomas. It appeared that Maurice was in conversation with Thomas, who, inside of the house, was holding a revolver to his own head. Thomas didn't have any clothes on and was acting very irrationally.

Using a bullhorn I attempted to talk with the disturbed young man, but it was to no avail. I put the bullhorn down and proceeded very carefully to the front door of the Haley residence. I knew that Thomas could pull the trigger at any moment. Upon arrival at the scene, Bill Haley had told me that his brother Mark and Mrs. Haley were at their summer cottage up on the St. Lawrence River in the north country.

As I reached the front steps of the house, I became very concerned. I was afraid, but I managed to say a couple of prayers. I wondered, "Is this the end of my career? Will Thomas shoot himself? Will Thomas shoot me?" I remembered when Thomas was fourteen years old. I remembered that it was fourteen years ago, as I parked in my Troop Car, when Thomas approached me on his bicycle and we chatted about police work and how his aunt and uncle were soon to open their ice cream bar in Nedrow.

I thought about my sons and about my divorce and remarriage. I could very well be approaching the end of my life. I tried to put those sad memories behind me. I glanced over at the other officers on the scene, and my eyes focused on Maurice near the window and Thomas standing just inside holding that loaded and cocked revolver to his head.

The Haley home was a beautiful combination wood-and-stone house, the kind of residence that an executive would own. Mark Haley had been a very successful farmer and engineer. He, like his son Thomas after him, had graduated from Syracuse University. The family was well known in the Nedrow community. It was very evident that Maurice with the Sheriff's and me with the State Police would attempt to save Thomas from self-destruction or from being gunned down. It was a fragile moment in all three of our lives.

As I crossed over into the interior of the Haley home, I noticed on the floor by the front door a rifle and a makeshift barricade. Thomas was now standing in front of me in the nude, with the cocked revolver pressed against his right temple. He had moved from the window to meet me. He asked me if I were John Briant. It had been many years since I had seen Thomas. I told him that I was and asked him if we could talk about things.

Still holding the cocked revolver, he told me to take a seat. The seat was near the front window, and I could view Maurice. Thomas sat down in front of me across the table, still holding the cocked revolver to his head. His eyes looked wild, and my mind raced in an attempt to grasp the reality of the dangerous situation.

We talked about Nedrow, about the people. I could tell that he wasn't thinking clearly. He told me that he had been hurt in an accident on a sugar plantation located in the Hawaiian Islands. He told me that he had hit his head. After several minutes of low-keyed conversation, I asked him if he would allow Maurice Touhey to come into the house so the three of us could talk. To my great relief, Thomas agreed, and Maurice came into the house very cautiously. I looked at Maurice and Maurice looked at me. We tried to communicate with our eyes as to what we were going to do next.

Thomas still held the revolver with the muzzle pressed against his right temple. He frequently waved the revolver through the air placing the muzzle in his mouth and back to his right temple. Both of us officers felt compassion for this young man who seemed so confused and not in control of his faculties. We suggested to Thomas the possibility of the three of us going to the Nedrow Tavern for a cold beer and further conversation. To our surprise, Thomas agreed to the plan.

We told him that it would be advisable to get dressed. Thomas, still in control of the revolver, walked to the other end of the living room and put on his trousers and shirt. We were just about ready to make the journey to the Tavern. Thomas asked us to place one blanket around our shoulders. Perhaps he thought that the blanket would give him a sense of security.

The three of us exited through the front door and walked slowly to the sidewalk. We crossed Salina Street and proceeded north along the sidewalk. Near the Nedrow Post Office was a wall. Thomas still held the revolver, fully cocked, to his right temple. He had also brought an ocarina (musical wind instrument) with him. I had brought a bottle of vermouth from the house. The three of us sat down on the wall. Maurice and I exchanged glances, trying to communicate to each other when to make the move toward Thomas. We did not want to hurt him in any way, but just get the gun away from him. The three of us talked some more about the cold beer they served at the Nedrow Tavern.

The time had come to start toward the Nedrow Tavern. Thomas had placed the loaded cocked revolver in the waistband of his trousers. Crowds of people had gathered, but were kept back a good distance. Thomas didn't notice the gathering crowds. We were in the middle of South Salina Street when I looked at Maurice and gave him a slight nod. Maurice read my mind. I grabbed for the revolver in Thomas's waistband, and Maurice quickly grabbed Thomas's arms. As my hand touched the revolver, I prayed that the movement would not discharge the weapon. It didn't. The crisis was over. The crowd cheered! The most important thing was that Maurice and I had saved the life of a twenty-eight-year old engineer. Thomas was taken to a private hospital for an evaluation. Maurice and I did have a beer together.

I often reflect on how the revolver was still cocked when I retrieved it from Haley's waistband. With the hammer cocked, the weapon could have discharged if it had been dropped or handled roughly, and it contained two live rounds of .32 Caliber ammunition. One of the rounds was in the firing position, and I am grateful to God that the trigger was not pulled during those crucial moments of suspense and uncertainty. Maurice and I were doing our job, and we both thanked God for giving us the courage and strength to bring a tense situation to a final conclusion without injury to anyone.

The reason that Thomas had called out my name was his memory of me sitting in my Troop Car, talking to him and other children in the Nedrow area many years ago. He associated my name with the word "help." I was happy that I was there for him.

*   *   *

On November 9, 1971, I was at home when the telephone rang at approximately seven o'clock in the evening. It was the North Syracuse Station. The dispatcher informed me that the State Police were on the Onondaga Indian Reservation investigating an alleged homicide. The Troopers at the scene requested my attendance.

All the time I was en route to the reservation I was wondering why I hadn't been called before. I was the one who had spent almost seventeen years working on the reserve. The State Police personnel at the scene knew that I was acquainted with the entire Indian population. Yet they had waited until now to call me. I let my feelings pass as I pulled into the area of the murder scene.

I soon learned that the victim of this brutal killing was a personal friend of mine. Chapman ("Chappy") Schandoah, a World War II veteran, was approximately sixty years of age at the time and resided in his home, which was located on the reservation behind the Salina Street Drive-In Theater. He was employed at the Valley Bakery located on South Salina Street, Syracuse.

I had only been at the scene for a few minutes when I was informed by a uniformed Trooper that a patrol had stopped Chappy's car near the dam, which is located on the southern end of the reservation. I proceeded to the dam and immediately observed the suspect killers. The shooter was fourteen years of age, an Indian youth known to me. I immediately identified myself to him and asked him to accompany me to my car. I was joined by a State Police commissioned officer.

The youth was advised of the Miranda warning. I told him, "You have the right to remain silent. For anything you say can be used against you in a court of law. You have the right to an attorney now or at any stage of the proceedings. Do you understand the rights that I have explained to you?"

He replied. "Yes, I understand."

I continued. "Having these rights in mind, do you wish to talk to us now?" "Yes." He responded.

"Did you shoot Chappy?" I asked.

"Yes." He said. After the officer and I obtained the confession, the three of us proceeded to the LaFayette barracks.

The investigation into the brutal slaying of Chapman revealed that three youths had entered his home and proceeded to commit a burglary. They removed two long arms from the home: a rifle and a shotgun. Nothing else had been taken. After committing the burglary they decided to wait outside the house until Chappy returned home from his job at the bakery. The youths knew Chappy.

The three youths watched Chappy come home and park his car. They watched him eat his supper and prepare to do the dishes in the kitchen sink. The killer then took the shotgun and fired through the window directly at Chappy, killing him instantly.

The killer then went inside the house for the second time and removed the car keys from the dead man's trousers' pocket. The three youths then stole Chappy's car, planning to go to New York City. But when they stopped at the dam located on the reservation to plan their trip to New York, a police car encountered them.

The outcome of the case was decided in Onondaga County Family Court. The shooter received three years in a youth-detention facility because of his age at the time of the killing.

He was released after two and one half years, and after a short time was arrested again for a vicious assault on an elderly Syracuse female resident with a screwdriver.

This case was a tragedy for the victim as well as the perpetrator. It is just one of the many incidents that occur in America every day of the week. I had personal knowledge of this particular youth's background. He belonged to a family where alcohol was consumed to an excess by both parents. It seemed to me, as an outside observer, that the young man didn't have a chance to grow up in an environment conducive to proper development.

During my tenure of working with the troubled youth of our district, I observed that those displaying deviant behavior were not just from a culture of poverty, but also from higher socio-economic families. This truth surfaced even more noticeably as the tentacles of the drug culture exercised their venom through the lives of many people.

Many of us in the police service have a great concern for our society's youth, and it is very disturbing to witness "kids" on a self-destructing course. It is so important for all of us to give of ourselves for the purpose of possibly making a difference.

Even though I am no longer an active member of the Division of State Police, I am still reminded of that little extra effort I put forth for our youth in those golden years of my career. Every so often a person will come up to me in a shopping mall or another place where the public gathers, and express their "thanks" for taking that extra moment with them during their formative years. At my official retirement celebration, several who came to the event, those youths now matured, expressed their appreciation to me for my advice and guidance that were shared with them during their climb up "fools" hill. I thanked them and told them that it was a healthy exchange and, above all, that we had learned from each other.

The month of February 1971 will always shine in my thoughts. As a result of the Thomas Haley incident in Nedrow I became a candidate for the highest award given to a State Police member regardless of rank or position. Mr. and Mrs. Brummer, wealthy Wall Street financiers, established a special account in an Albany bank from which the recipient of the award received the interest on the principle.

Although I didn't consider myself a hero for my participation in saving Mr. Haley from committing suicide, I did consider it my sworn duty to proceed with the actions I took toward the apprehension of Mr. Haley and keeping him from doing harm to himself. I will always be grateful to Onondaga County Sheriff's Detective Maurice Touhey for his role in the action taken. Without him it could have concluded in another way. We were very fortunate in the outcome.

During that second month of 1971 my wife and I were driven to Albany for the coveted Brummer Award presentation. My Troop Commander, Raymond Rassmussen, was our chauffeur, accompanied by my BCI Supervisor, Captain George Dana.

The award was presented to me at the New York State Police

Academy in the presence of two hundred recruits attending the Academy. It was an honor that will always warm my thoughts. I was given the privilege of speaking to the new Trooper candidates. I told them that I was receiving this award not just for myself, but for the entire Division of State Police. I further told them that possibly someday while serving in their chosen career, they, too, might become involved in an incident where the going would be a little "rough." I assured them that they were in the process of receiving some of the best police training in the world, and in the event they had to face future danger they would be ready to do their sworn duty.

Receiving the Brummer Award was one of the highlights of my career. This is an appropriate time to thank my senior man, Alfred Secor, who has since passed away, but will never be forgotten. Trooper Secor shared his knowledge with me during the initial phases of my recruit training. He possessed "wisdom" and "know-how" and was a most dedicated member of Troop D. Trooper Secor went on to become Technical Sergeant Secor before he retired. As I have said, Al and Grace Secor gave much of their selves to the early days of my career.

The Brummer Award was followed with two others that I received as a result of the Haley incident.

During May of the same year I received the U.S. Army Medal of Valor Award from the 1209th Army Reserve Unit Assigned to Mattydale. This award was presented in the presence of several government notables, family and friends. The ceremony was most impressive and will always remain in my memory.

The third award I received concerning the Haley incident was the National Exchange Club Award, sponsored by the Unity Insurance Company. The plaque displayed the words "For Outstanding Devotion to Duty and Meritorious Service to the Community." U.S. Senator Patrick Moynihan attended the award ceremony.

I was honored to have received these awards during my State Police Service, and I will always be. But again, I never considered myself a hero. I was doing the job I was sworn to do. However, like anything else, there is another side to the coin. The awards are symbols of appreciation by one's peers, and even though they are rightly deserved, they also place one in an awkward position. The recipient always feels that he or she has to serve above and beyond the call of duty. The person also becomes a target. Let's take the historic "wild west days" of America. When a fast gun came to a town, there was always some other fast gun out there to offer a challenge. In my case, fast guns were not the problem. I always felt pressured to do more. It was frustrating to observe unproductive people getting promoted, while I was being continually overlooked.

It is not my intention to delve into the organizational procedures of promotion. I do, however, feel that hard working producers should have a share of the promotion pie. Again, in my own case, as Station Commander, I was required to participate in hours and hours of administrative functions, doing the work of a Sergeant while receiving Trooper's pay. This practice was unfair not only to me, but to others as well. Fortunately the work scene has changed a great deal since the fifties and sixties. Very seldom is a Senior Trooper placed in charge of a Station. Now there is a special signifying rank for Station Commanders. The young people of any organization today demand and receive these privileges, unlike the work force of the fifties and sixties, who struggled on with their job pressures.

*   *   *

I stayed in touch with my sons as much as possible, but it was difficult to travel to Massachusetts. Sometimes I went to see them and, after driving two hundred and fifty miles, I found them not home. It presented a dilemma. Unless someone lives through not having your sons with them, they cannot know the deep-seated pain that is continually piercing one's heart and soul.

Mary and I did our best in our marriage. Both of us continued to work hard at our jobs. Both of us knew many people in our area in the southern part of Onondaga County. The people in the towns and hamlets were always gracious to us. Even the local people whom I had to arrest over the years were civil to us and never showed us anything but respect.

It was during an assigned State Fair detail in 1973 that I met Investigator Melvin Nemier. Mel, assigned to Troop "B" Malone, worked with me for the ten days of Fair week. I learned that he was originally from Sandy Creek, New York, where he had taught music in a high school prior to entering the State Police. He learned that I was in my twentieth year as a member of the Troopers.

At one point during our conversations, Mel informed me that

there was an opening for an investigator in his troop. I had told him that one of my desires was to be assigned to the North country of New York. Mel told me that he would check into it and let me know about the open slot for investigator.

After the State Fair Detail ended, Mel returned to Malone. A few days went by, and then I received a telephone call from him. He informed me that if I were interested in a transfer to Troop "B," that I should put in for it. I followed Mel's suggestions. The transfer was approved at Division Headquarters, and Mary and I made our plans for the move. We were both excited about it.

During the latter part of November 1973 we sold our mobile home. It was not easy leaving our valley after several years of enjoying the scenic beauty that it offered. We had, nevertheless, made up our minds to transfer to the adventurous north country of New York State. The decision was not made without reservation; however, my workplace was becoming more and more difficult.

My eighteen years in the LaFayette district had threaded my professional life with rich and meaningful relationships with the majority of the people. But it had become apparent to me that the networking of meaningful contacts that I had labored so hard to form and maintain was becoming frayed. Some of my associates definitely resented me, and this attitude spun out into the public mainstream. My inner self dictated this move that I was about to make.

The situation at work became very repulsive to me. There comes a time in everyone's life when enough is enough. I had been raised in a family where love and respect for our fellow human being was well-defined. The harassment by some of my coworkers intensified. Childish notes appeared in my mail folder. There were many phone calls to my residence with clicks in my ear when I answered. These actions kept me in a state of agitation.

During this time of my life I tried to figure out why this was happening. I had dedicated my life to the division. To keep my position in perspective, I had never forgotten the behavior of organizations and the people within them. I debated internally for hours, but I came to no satisfying conclusion about my dilemma. So I was determined to look forward to the new challenges that faced Mary and me in the North Country.

Prior to our move, in the fall of 1973, we purchased a brand new mobile home from a dealership in Malone. It was seventy feet long and twelve feet wide. The rustic interior created an aura of coziness. Both of us fell in love with this new home.

The park in which we placed the home was located in Moira. We had selected an end lot with adequate privacy. The owner of the park, Robert Baker (who insisted we call him "Bob"), was a self-employed contractor in the Moira area. He greeted us with a sincerely warm attitude. He was a person whom others instantly liked.

Mary told me that she would like to go to work a few hours a week. She checked the local papers and found nothing suitable. In the early winter of 1973, Mary was hired by the Malone School District as a teacher's aide. She found the work interesting.

My first day at work was a day of indoctrination in Troop "B." I met the Troop Commander, Donald Ambler, for whom I had previously worked in Troop D. He welcomed me to the district.

Investigator Melvin Nemier briefed me on my responsibilities and assigned me a car. I met the BCI Captain and Lieutenant and the rest of the BCI unit. They all seemed pleased to have me aboard.

In order to become familiar with the Troop "B" Headquarters BCI district, I rode with Mel and other Investigators for about a two-week period.

The land area surrounding the Malone barracks was rather flat, and a person had to drive several miles south on Route 30 to see any change in terrain. It was a beautiful area. The leaves had fallen from the trees, and I could sense that the winter of 1973 was just around the corner. It did not take long to learn the district.

The BCI Captain, Fred Teeple, was a seasoned officer with plenty of wisdom and a good sense of humor. He told me several times, "Keep your gas tank filled, for we have a large area here and you could run out of gasoline." I listened to the Captain, and I soon realized that his suggestion was on target. Many times during my assignment to Malone the gas tank was operating on fumes when I pulled up in front of the barracks pump.

Usually at lunchtime we would go to the A & W Root Beer stand and enjoy the chili dogs. On Tuesdays they sold for twenty-six cents apiece. Often we would consume five or six of these tasty chili-covered dogs. The stand served diet root beer, and I clearly remember the frosty glasses they served it in. What a treat!!

We had similar investigations. Burglaries of camps, homes and barns occurred regularly. Natural deaths seemed common during the winter months. Many of these deaths were of people residing alone in small homes. It was sad to imagine the last days of these lonely people, many of them elderly, who lived by themselves. Sometimes we were notified of these unattended deaths by the mail carrier.

The incidents of firearm use in crimes seemed high for a rural territory. During my tenure at Troop "B," several homicides and armed robberies took place. The BCI Units of Troop "B" were most efficient, and the members worked very well together. I was happy to be a part of this hard working group of people.

Mary enjoyed her job at the school in Malone. She worked about four days a week. The teachers treated her very well, and she developed an excellent relationship with the school children.

I was invited to attend a magistrate association dinner held at the Crossroads Restaurant in Moira. I guess this dinner was our "official" welcome to the area. I was allowed to say a few words to the group, so I told them some of my experiences while I was assigned to Troop "D." The participants were very cordial, and the dinner and the program was a success.

Snowmobiling was popular in the region during the winter months. Mary and I had our own sleds. We did most of our riding in the Santa Clara area, located just east of St. Regis Falls. Trails sparkled like newly polished diamonds when the sun's rays hit the snow. The crisp noise of the sled's tracks slicing through the pure white added to the adventure. Welcome part of snowmobiling, a lunch of tasty hot dogs (buried in a roll with relish and mustard) satisfied our taste buds. A sip of peach brandy warmed our fingertips. After this treat we would again strike out for a remote area of the region. The snowmobile culture brought people together for plenty of chatter, brandy, and friendly vying to see what sled would perform the best.

Mary and I joined a snowmobile club in Canada and another in Malone. They provided adventure in our off duty hours of the winter season. We continued to return to the Santa Clara area as well as Canada.

The two Ski Doos we owned functioned very well. The flat land offered an adequate proving ground to test the sleds for their speed and durability. The only problems we experienced were a blown spark plug on one trip and a worn-out driving belt on another.

During our visits to Quebec we met many people enjoying the sport of snowmobiling. One family in particular whom we came to know on a social basis were the Tessiers. Several years before I had met Claude Tessier, a barber for 20 years, from the Syracuse area. He told me about his mother and father who resided in Dewittville, Quebec.

The Tessier family were gracious hosts, and on our visits to their home we were treated to a variety of French cuisine. Claude would join us at his parents' when he was in the area. The occasions were always festive.

Claude's father, who was in his late seventies at the time, told us often of his many challenges during the eighteen years as the champion arm wrestler of the Province of Quebec. As a lumberjack in his younger days, he had cut timber in the Forestport, New York, area. Later, after working vigorously on the Tessier farm during the week, he would take a train to Montreal to meet his challenger. He maintained the championship well into his fifties before he was finally beaten by a thirty-year-old. The senior Tessier was a large man who had always worked hard all through his life. Even in his late seventies his hand grip was pulverizing if he decided to apply the pressure.

During our snowmobile rides in eighteen-degrees-below-zero temperatures, Ivan Tessier, Claude's father, would wear only a leather snowmobile hat without a face mask. Everyone else was bundled up with face shields and scarves wrapped around their necks and heads. Our jaunts across the frozen terrain would bring us to small hamlets, and we liked to stop at the various pubs to listen to the music and chatter about the frigid snowmobile ride. Ivan sat at the table like a huge giant and sang French songs to the group. It was a memorable time for everyone. There was no talk about politics nor any discussion that would tend to distract our attention from the gala time we enjoyed with our neighbors from Quebec.

The fellowship with our Canadian friends was very important to us. We discussed the differences in our countries, and talked about the cultures, and soon learned they were similar. They were family oriented. They worked hard at their jobs, and looked forward to their leisure time;

much like their American counterparts. These times were a learning experience. We also talked about culinary skills, such as preparation of pepper steak and the correct way to make a meat pie. Sipping Ivan's homemade wine always led to more singing, too.

Charles Taylor, Claude's brother-in-law, who worked for Cornell University on the Brown Estate as a marine biologist, joined us on these journeys. I remember Charley's family very well. His wife was Claude's sister, who was a county nurse in New York State. She took care of any bodily abrasions that occurred on the trips. Charley's good friend, William Brown (of Brown's Sound Inc. in Syracuse), was a most pleasant chap who added his wisdom and storytelling talents to the campfire get-togethers.

During the mid-1970's we enjoyed several large-group snow-mobile journeys in the Santa Clara area located in Franklin County in upstate New York. This very quaint hamlet was not very populated, but a visitor could tell that life did exist there by the smoke swirling from the chimneys. We would stop at the Santa Clara Hotel operated by Mrs. Collins. She and her husband ran the hotel for fifty years prior to the mid-70's, and after her husband's death she continued to serve the public. The hotel was old and rustic, with about twenty rooms and a large kitchen. Our snowmobile group stayed there several times.

The breakfast that Fannie Collins served was a special event by itself. The sizzling bacon and fresh eggs on the hot grill sent an aroma that would galvanize anyone's taste buds. The brown-golden home fries and thick-cut succulent ham slices captured everyone's attention. Butter-topped pancakes finally softened the pangs of hunger. Final cups of hot coffee, accompanied by home-baked cinnamon rolls topped with vanilla glaze, completed the breakfast event.

For our trail ride Fannie prepared paper-bag lunches (a sand-wich, an apple and a cookie) which held us through the day until supper time. We all wondered how this lady of over eighty years in age could manage the pressures connected with food preparation. Dedication to real culinary art for the public is rare these days; many talented ladies such as Fannie Collins have passed away, and the junk food of the present time will never offer the quality of the fare we so enjoyed as guests of the Santa Clara Hotel.

There were other adventures Mary and I enjoyed in the North

Country experience. Boating, fishing the fresh lakes, hiking, and tramping through the woods were just some of the good times.

In 1974 a new member of the family joined us: a six-month-old Alaskan Malamute with papers. We named him "Brianna of Widmere." Gray, black and white, Brianna had a beautiful face; he actually smiled showing his white sharp teeth. A lively dog, he required a lot of care.

I was kept busy at the Malone barracks and worked mostly around the western part of the district: Hopkinton, Nicholville, St. Regis Falls, Santa Clara, Brasher Falls and Lawrenceville. It didn't take long to meet people in the area. They were fine folks, but at first were a little hesitant to give forth very much information about any criminal activity in their areas. It took a few months to "break the ice," but I managed to close several good cases while I was there in the district.

In the latter part of 1974 my marriage of ten years took a different direction. Mary and I became distant as our feeling toward each other began to deteriorate. The rift caused us both pain. The usual "tongue wagging" started in the community. People who should have been minding their own business seemed more interested in ours. Rumors circulated in this small community.

Mary and I talked for hours in an attempt to resolve our feelings. During the final days of our relationship we mutually agreed to divorce. The situation was shocking to both of us. Unless someone has gone through the process themselves no one can understand the turmoil that takes place within oneself. Neither of us was completely to blame, and we both suffered much heartache.

Anyone in public service who gets divorced sustains damage beyond belief. One's life is not one's own. One is judged by peers continually, and the magnifying inquiries made by management behind one's back are embarrassing to both spouses. Mary and I rose above the malicious gossip, however, and continued with the process.

When the divorce was over I was left with a mobile home containing one bed, a table with four chairs, my clothes, my job and a broken heart. I gave Brianna away to a good home. For a while I endured a state of real depression. My bitterness was somewhat softened by the fact that even though we were now divorced, Mary and I maintained a mutual respect for each other. And though the tongues kept on wagging, in a short while they were making a target of someone else.

Within a year I married Denise, a widow. I signed a pre-nuptial agreement that would prohibit my benefiting from her estate. The marriage was happy for about six months until her children began putting undue stress on our relationship. A lot of pressure was applied to both of us. Her son, who lived home, appeared full of rage and began drinking to excess. Denise became concerned. Her daughter left home. She was going with an older man. Denise became consumed with guilt, believing she was to blame because of our marriage.

In the midst of this turmoil, the State Police transferred me to the Massena barracks, approximately twenty miles away. This transfer added to my dilemma. The Massena Station was a busy place. I spent a great deal of time handling investigations on the St. Regis Indian Reservation. The Indians were predominantly Mohawk, and many of them were relatives to the Onondagas in Nedrow.

While assigned to Massena I worked on several homicide cases and other important issues that came to our attention. My job had always been important to me, and now it became even more so. The impending demise of my personal life left me distraught and confused. Love's end is tragic, and it had happened to me. I had never intended to become a divorced person, and here I was in 1976 at age 46 with only a box full of awards for outstanding police dedication and service to the communities that I had so faithfully served.

I did not seek a divorce at the time of my transfer to Massena, however our relationship continued to deteriorate. Eventually, Denise and I became legally separated. My third marriage was crumbling.

My personal life continued to be an open wound. I would never recommend to anyone this life's path that I pursued. It was a trip of despair that brought humiliation in just about every facet of my life.

It was difficult for me to believe that my personal life had brought me three failed marriages. To place the blame on myself wholly would not be correct, and to place the blame on my three spouses would be as equally incorrect. I was not searching for excuses to eliminate my self-blame. I didn't want to blame the love for the job as a Trooper. It happened. As I continue on from 1976 I will further illustrate to the reader other things that can occur in a lifetime after three marriages.

In 1976 I requested a transfer back to Troop "D". The transfer was approved and I was ordered to report to Troop "D" Headquarters to meet with the Troop Commander. The Commander was new to central New York and had just taken command of Troop "D."

The interview lasted for about an hour. He advised me that he had reviewed my personnel file and was aware of my job productivity. However, he went on to tell me, that he had received some telephone calls from some of the members with whom I had worked. They had indicated to the Major that I was indeed a trouble-maker. With barely controlled anger I asked the Major to bring forth these pious heroes who sat in judgement of me on my returning to Troop "D". I assured the Major that I was not a person who initiated trouble. I refrained from telling him of the repeated harassment I endured prior to transferring to Troop "B".

I continued my interview with the Major. I went into my family background and described my good relationship with my parents and siblings. During the interview, I had the definite impression that the force would have been pleased to accept my notice of retirement. This was another blow to me. Now my career that had meant so much to me was being challenged. The message was clear in that interview room in 1976: either bring forth my accusers face to face, or refrain from this degrading interview. The Major agreed that the negative telephone calls he had received were groundless: however, there were affirmative calls received that stood firm in my behalf. The Major concluded the interview and advised me that he would be in touch with me. I thanked the Major and left the room.

In a two-week period I was assigned to State Police, Lowville: a three-man BCI Unit and several uniformed personnel. The area, part of Lewis County, was basically an agriculture region. Its main routes were 12, 12D, 26 and 812.

The crimes that occurred consisted of burglary, robbery, lower grades of larceny, and criminal mischief to property. In addition, there were always fatal and serious personal-injury accidents along with many property-damage accidents.

During the winter of 1976, the snowbanks were twenty feet high in front of my apartment in the hamlet of Turin. This area is a part of the Tug Hill plateau, and the weather patterns bring many heavy snowfalls. Turin, well-known for skiing, draws people from all over New York State and Canada. A U.S. Army ski team uses the slopes in their training exercises. The scenery in the area is eye catching during all seasons.

After I had completed one year of service in the Lowville district, I successfully applied for another transfer, this time to State Police, North Syracuse.

That same year, 1977, a telephone call from my attorney informed me that my divorce from my third wife was final. The time period of one year separation had been met, whereby a final divorce decree had been granted to me by the Supreme Court of New York State.

In the same time period I found it necessary to file for bankruptcy. Debts had accumulated. I had made arrangements with several of my creditors to pay off some of my debts. These included two bank loans. A payment schedule had been arranged. Everyone should use sound judgement in using credit cards and borrowing money. Credit card use to an excess can be costly. One's credit rating can be put into jeopardy. This can initiate more tongue-wagging by co-workers and former friends. Filing for bankruptcy should be avoided, if possible. One should attempt other alternatives in handling financial difficulties.

My duties from 1977 to 1982, while assigned to the North Syracuse barracks, introduced me to the crimes of fraud, forgery, and embezzlement. Even though I had investigated the so-called white-collar crime at a previous station assignment, I now found myself working on this type of case exclusively. The senior investigator in charge of the North Syracuse BCI unit had approached me with the idea of assigning a man to this specialty. Although I suspected this plan was a veiled way of keeping me out of the limelight, I did not object to the proposed assignment and agreed to his suggestion.

The work was exciting. I handled every forgery case that was brought to our attention. I spent a considerable time visiting the banking community in Onondaga County, and assisting their security people with the criminal prosecution of many of the cases. Sometimes I had to travel to other cities within the state. The forgery schemes that were perpetrated were cleverly planned, and each case of this nature required intense research and planning to bring about a criminal action. Many times the cases were presented directly to the Grand Jury, which would listen to the evidence being presented by bank and institution employees and me. Usually an indictment followed the Grand Jury process.

I always maintained that if the forger or embezzler used their talents for something good, they would become very successful people in a legitimate field of endeavor. Some of the schemes were ingenious. The hungry greed that inspires this criminal activity is powerful and can be very damaging to the person(s) involved in its creation as well as to the victim(s) of the scheme. In this complex society of the twentieth century, people should be aware of the fraud and con-artist. Aside from the harm done directly to the victims, it is this type of criminal activity that increases our insurance premiums. Anyone suspecting activity of this nature should immediately notify the authorities.

Another interesting point is that people involved in the crime of forgery are some of the most desperate criminals. One such case comes to mind. On a cold spring day in the late seventies, Security Officer Terry Conners accompanied me to a residence on the south side of Syracuse in an effort to interview a subject who was suspected of stealing business checks from a beauty school. The suspect had forged the endorsement of the school president and acquired funds amounting to over a thousand dollars. We did not locate the man at home.

In the two days that followed, the same suspect assaulted a nurse at a Syracuse Hospital and fled the city. Within the following week this suspect murdered a New Jersey woman. He was subsequently arrested for the homicide in New Jersey. This case illustrates that forgers are not always "civilized" people but can display hostility and violence and become involved in major crimes.

I think back to the day that Mr. Conners and I attempted to interview the suspect. If we had located him, our mindset would have been to make a casual inquiry about a forged endorsement check. But what might he have done to us? The victim in New Jersey was murdered by a gun.

The growing drug culture has greatly increased the incidence of forgery and embezzlement, as addicts and frequent users turn to these crimes to acquire the funds to buy more drugs.

When going out for an evening of social activity, a person should be careful where they hang their pocketbooks or their jackets containing their wallets. Many times during a forgery investigation it is learned that the checkbook or credit cards had been stolen from a woman's purse while she left it hanging on the back of a barstool or chair. The criminal can then obtain money or services by forging the checks and forging the credit card owner's name to sales slips. As a result of this type of criminal activity, millions of dollars are stolen each year.

While assigned to State Police North Syracuse I became a member of the International Association of Credit Card Investigators (IACCI). This organization conducts meetings on a monthly basis and offers an excellent insight to the business world. Many exchanges among the numerous members have struck a blow to the villains who perpetrate the frauds. This networking relationship helps to counter a serious attack on individuals and the business establishment.

IACCI was similar to another organization to which I had belonged, while assigned to Troop "B": the St. Lawrence Law Enforcement Association, through which law enforcement people from the United States met law enforcement agencies from Canada on a monthly basis. The dinner meetings were usually held in Cornwall, Ontario, and provided for a friendly exchange of information that benefited the Canadian and the United States Law Enforcement communities. The results of these meetings over the years have dealt a severe blow to the criminal element on both sides of the U.S. and Canadian borders.

I rented a room in the Tully area for several months upon my return to Troop "D." Later on my residence became a small motel cabin in LaFayette. It was a very difficult existence to live alone without family and a limited number of friends. I learned that when a person is in a downward spiral, there are some people who enjoy the continuation of vicious attacks. It wasn't easy; however, I held my ground and with God's assistance survived the tumultuous ordeal that gradually lessened. The people responsible will always know unto themselves what they endeavored to accomplish in the attempted destruction of a human being.

I went to Massachusetts on several occasions to visit my sons. John was a member of the United States Air Force. He was also attending college on a part-time basis. James had now established himself working in the maintenance department of a high school. When I did see them it was an enjoyable time. The frequency of these visits diminished upon my return to Troop "D" as they pursued their own lives with their mother and stepfather.

The visits to my mother during this time were infrequent because of my work responsibilities. We talked on the telephone and exchanged letters twice a month.

My brother and his family still resided in Arizona. Besides

working every day at General Electric and later Honeywell, he maintained a position with Glendale Community College as a teacher of advertising and office management. I had taken several trips to the sunshine state, starting in 1967. Anyone who has visited the southwest is aware of the intense heat during the summertime. I find it a beautiful state to visit, but knew the heat would be difficult for me to adjust to on a longtime basis.

I had very little social life during this time in my life. I worked a lot of afternoon shifts from three o'clock in the afternoon until eleven o'clock in the evening. I found it a good time to catch the forgers and embezzlers; sometimes they were in the middle of their evening meal at the time of apprehension—often eating good food that was paid for by theft.

My love for music was ever present. One evening I stopped after work to listen to a well-known musical group. It was on this particular night that I became reacquainted with a lady whom I had previously met years ago at the funeral of a mutual friend. At this second meeting I learned that she danced very well. Her name was Margie. That evening after the dance was over, we went to the local Howard Johnson's Restaurant. Over corn muffins and hot coffee we began a friendship of a quality that I had never experienced before in my life.

We exchanged ideas on everything from children to politics. In the months that ensued, we enjoyed picnics, attended weddings of friends, consumed a great many Heid's hot dogs, went on camping trips, and danced every chance we could find. It was an excellent friendship. Neither one of us wanted marriage; it was the farthest thing from our minds. She would listen to my sorrow as I poured it out to her about my three marriages and three divorces, difficult issues to discuss. She patiently stood by me in moments of frustration. I shared with her some of the bitterness that spills over from an organization that permits blatant harassment and unjust labeling. She shared the sadness she experienced with the death of her husband and the trials and tribulations of a female's struggle in a male dominated work environment where she was a specialist in the computer field of the General Electric Company. After the verbal exchange, both of us realized how fortunate it was for our lives to cross again. She was one of the most intelligent persons whom I had ever met and very attractive.

On one visit to my motel home she asked me, "Why are you torturing yourself?" The room, I admit, was small and damp. The shower head didn't work properly and the roof leaked. She persuaded me to look for a better place to live.

We looked together. Finally we located a large one-room efficiency apartment on James Street in Syracuse. I can remember some of the meals that I took pride in preparing for her. A favorite we both enjoyed was the hot sausage patties smothered in a rich tomato sauce with green peppers, onions and plenty of garlic. Sometimes we would open up a bottle of vintage wine to accompany our delicacy.

We spent many off-duty times in our favorite place, "The Adirondack Park." It was a place where peace and quiet existed. A place where the deer came over for a piece of bread and the ducks sat along the shoreline of a fresh water lake. It was a place where our affection grew for one another without the cruelty of the critics.

Our friendship was just short of two years by three months when intrusive peer pressure was exerted on both of us by the children. It immediately brought back memories of my third marriage. Marge and I discussed the issues involved and mutually agreed to part. The separation lasted three months. It was a hell on earth. During this time I harangued myself and wondered savagely who had the right to cause such conflict that brought about this torment. I had strong feelings that people should keep their noses out of other people's private lives. Hey! This was still America, the land of freedom, and I didn't hear that the rules had been changed!

I meditated some more and finally on a cold day in January of 1979, I called Margie on the telephone. We talked and talked. I asked her on the phone, Will you marry me? The silence was scary. She finally spoke. "Yes I will. When?"

On January 26, 1979, in the presence of six friends, we were united in marriage, officiated by the Honorable Helen Burnham, Town Justice, of the Town of Salina.

During the first four months of our marriage we rented a small house on the south side of Syracuse, in a neighborhood with which I was thoroughly familiar. The house had a fireplace. The applewood that we burned could be appreciated by the whole neighborhood, as its pleasant aroma entered everyone's house for two blocks around.

In February of 1979 we travelled to Arizona to meet my brother and his family. I took Marge to some of the scenic areas around Phoenix. We spent a few days in the hills of Prescott, northwest of Phoenix. While there we ate at a local restaurant. We will always remember that lunch and its aftermath. I had ordered cabbage salad, but didn't realize as I was eating it that the dressing was spoiled. My body's reaction began that evening at a motel in Williams. Fierce stomach pains started at about nine-thirty in the evening, and I didn't recover until two days later. Because of this unexpected event there was a change in plans. It had been our intention to visit the south rim of the Grand Canyon; however we never did reach our destination, for snow came and it convinced us to return to the Phoenix area.

So the trip to Williams didn't work out the way we had planned. When we reached Phoenix I called David and told him what had happened. Then we turned our 1974 Ford E-200 south toward Tucson and then east from Tucson toward New Mexico and Texas. It was this trip that we considered our honeymoon. Fortunately we stayed on the southern travel routes as we continued eastward. When we stopped in Texas and had a muffler replaced, the garageman told us that we had just missed a hailstorm that had damaged several cars in the Abilene area.

In about five days we crossed the Pennsylvania-New York border. We were tired and glad to have returned to our home state.

We fell back into our daily work routine. Both Marge and I, as children raised during the Great Depression, had learned the hard work ethic at an early age. However, it was not easy surviving the dynamics within the organization. Behavior in the workplace was a different experience daily, and sometimes the policies changed on a minute-to-minute basis.

I can fully appreciate how my father felt about working for someone else. He had been a very dedicated and loyal employee in the various positions he held with the government and companies for which he worked. But it was his own Aunt Sarah's Fried Cake Bakery that brought a sense of peace to my father. He worked long hours in the bakery, but he didn't mind them; it was his own business, and he was "the Boss." He was well on his way to success when his health failed. My wife mentions every so often, when speaking of the good days in her early General Electric career, how she and her co-workers enjoyed dad's fried cakes, which sold in the vending machines in a small package, two for fifteen cents.

It has been very difficult for all of us since his passing. Even today as I humbly attempt to bring back the memories of my life through this keyboard I will never forget my dad, nor will I ever forget the best fried cake ever made, "Aunt Sarah's Potato Fried Cakes." There was no grease in dad's fried cakes. Today you can cross the country and try the fried cakes on the market and you will never locate a comparable fried cake.

In May of 1979 Marge and I purchased our first new home together: a Ryan Home, white with black trim. The raised ranch had a stately aura about it on its small lot. The two-car garage was a most welcome option. We converted one of the smaller bedrooms into a den. On the walls in neatly arranged frames were various awards and letters that pertained to my State Police career.

We designed our family room on the lower level and finished it off in knotty pine. We added a woodstove situated on a raised brick shelf. The bar consisted of a five-inch piece of pine, which we sanded, stained, and sealed with about seven coats of a clear varnish. Aged barnwood placed behind the bar created a western atmosphere, augmented with horseshoes, antique tools and badges from the old western days of the sheriffs and famous marshals. Our family room became a conversation piece. Numerous neighbors and some of my snowmobile friends would stop by to visit. It was a pleasant neighborhood. We enjoyed the area.

I can remember during a New York State Fair week, Marge made her special baked lasagna. Several of the BCI (Bureau of Criminal Investigation) came to the house, and what a feast we had. We were off duty. The red wine was smooth with the ample portions of lasagna, antipasto, garlic bread, and eggplant. The fellows must have been hungry, for there was nothing left over. It was one of my career days where there was a sense of real fellowship.

Along with my Forgery Detail assignment during 1980 I was fortunate to be assigned to the XIII Olympic Winter Games held at Lake Placid, New York from February 13, 1980 to February 24, 1980. The efforts and the accomplishments of the participating athletes from all over the world will always be in my memory.

My first assignment was to the Olympic Arena and after two days several of us were reassigned to the Athlete Bus Security from 6:00 AM

- 2:00 PM. We were responsible for the security of the athletes to and from the different venues of sport activity. The many athletes that I personally came in contact with exhibited warm friendliness, and showed a great deal of interest in our country.

Although my duty assignments took place in the Olympic Arena and on the Venue buses, I have to salute the Olympic State Police Detail and the Department of Environmental Conservation officers, who demonstrated their true professionalism in maintaining their calmness, courtesy and helpfulness in a sometimes stressful situation. The 1980 Olympic Detail was another highlight of my State Police career.

After the Olympics, work continued on my forgery cases. The cooperation I received from the banking community was excellent. As a result, many forgery cases were closed by arrest. The results of my dedicated efforts came to the forefront in May of 1980.

On May 4th, 1980, after a selection process, I became the recipient of the 10th Annual Harold Ross Memorial Award presented at the Tipperary Hill American Legion Post # 1361. A certificate and plaque accompanied the honor. The plaque contained the following:

"Presented to JOHN H. BRIANT for outstanding service to his community through carrying out his duties as a police officer in a manner which reflects credit upon all Law Enforcement Officers and for dedication to his profession above and beyond the call of duty."

It was a memorable event and I appreciated the award.

On May 15th, 1980, I received a letter from Melvin N. Zimmer, Assemblyman for the 120th District. The letter congratulated me for receiving the award. I will always remember and appreciate Assemblyman Zimmer's comments.

From 1980 to the third quarter of 1981 I continued to work my forgery cases—during this period of time, generally bank-stimulated cases. Forgers who targeted our area would often set up his/her scheme to defraud not only one bank, but several. Another organization that I belonged to was the Syracuse Clearing House Committee on Security, very helpful to me as I gathered important information on forgery schemes that were being perpetrated in the area. As a result of successful apprehensions of numerous white collar criminals on a day to day basis we were successful in stemming this type of criminal activity.

I continued to pursue my duties with vigor. I functioned alone in developing forgery cases for our North Syracuse BCI Unit. But again in my career I sensed some discontent among co-workers. This came in the form of getting the cold shoulder, curt answers to any question I might pose, not being included in conversations and a general attitude of unfriendliness. I was informed by some loyal associates that I might start to feel pressure from upper management. I passed this off and attempted to dismiss the warning, in hopes that my record could withstand criticism.

Unfortunately the warning I had received from my loyal associates became a reality during the fall of 1981. One Friday morning when I arrived at work, prior to leaving on my two-week vacation the following day, I was summoned to the office of my Senior Investigator. He began by announcing, "We may have a pattern developing here."

In that office I became a verbal target of that young man for whom I had a great deal of respect. He informed me that other members of my unit didn't feel that I was carrying my equal share of the workload. I could feel my blood pressure begin to surge. I angrily reminded the Senior that he had assigned me to the Forgery Squad and given me to understand that it was my duty assignment.

As I continued to sit there, I began to sense that the voice speaking was the Senior Investigator's, but his words were someone else's. My memory returned to what my loyal associates had forewarned me about.

This was my moment. I stood up and loudly and distinctly told the Senior, "I have always been a loyal employee and a dedicated Trooper. I am not going to sit here and be humiliated by you or anyone else." I had all I could do to control my left fist. I asked him, "Are you done?" What a way to send a person off on a two-week vacation.

It was at this turning point that I reflected back on my early years with the Division. The transfer to Herkimer from Waterloo. The hardship of reporting to Teletype duty once or twice a week. The miscarriages my wife had to endure without my presence. The harassment in the form of nasty notes left unsigned in my mail folder. The stalking by a fellow worker, who I startled on more than one occasion, when I accidentally reversed my direction. Then I remembered early on in my young career with joy when my (then) Zone Lieutenant Melvin Handville had told the upper management to get off this Trooper's butt.

I didn't want to retire, but I couldn't stand there in the Senior's office and swallow anymore of this bullshit -- there's no other word for it— I checked out on sick leave giving the reason of my hypertension for which I had been treated, and quietly said good-bye to the New York State Police. Enough was enough.

Readers, I want you all to know that leaving my job as a member of this fine law enforcement organization was one of the most difficult things that I ever had to do in my entire life.

The job that I had loved, dedicated my entire working life to, at the expense of my wives, my sons, my finances, now loomed before me as an impending loss. How was I to survive?

During the following six months I saw my physician on several occasions to be treated for high blood pressure. I suffered from mild depression as well during this period of time. My physician, not wishing to upset me, advised me that my supervisor had been to his office seeking information regarding my personal health record, which violates the patient/doctor relationship. He also indicated that these people were not my friends. My blood pressure continued to rise.

Lieutenant Edward Cass contacted me on several occasions to inform me that I did not have to retire and that I could return to duty if I so desired. I thanked him for his support, but told him that I had decided to officially retire from the State Police after twenty-eight years and four months of loyal and dedicated service. I had joined the ranks of the walking wounded.

V

Life After The New York State Police

V

It is deeply astonishing to a person who serves an organization for a long period of time when he or she is faced with the reality that the organization no longer wants him or her. I knew that if I returned to duty after six months on sick leave, the job would eventually become very devastating to me. I wanted to keep intact my pride: over those years my life had crossed the lives of thousands of citizens; I never abused my power to my fellow human being and was still able to close eighty-five percent of my cases by arrest.

So my expectations of becoming a Senior Investigator with the elite Bureau of Criminal Investigation never materialized. I had been a Station Commander in uniform for four years, and even though my station never exceeded fourteen members at any one time it was one of the leading patrol stations in the State, responsible for closing many excellent criminal cases. I knew I could lead a BCI unit, but apparently enough people in upper management had been so influenced by the rumor mongers that the promotion never came my way. I had always acted on the advice of my father: "Son, it is always beneficial for one to advance in their chosen profession, but never lower your ideologies of how to get from point A to point B." How sadly I learned that in this complex society very few people reach their goal without assistance from others. Because I could never lower my dignity to "kiss butt," my position as an investigator was a dead end one.

Marge was always there to support me emotionally during this time. After two months my depressed feelings subsided and I quit feeling sorry for myself, I sought another occupation.

I called Norman M. Goodfellow, Security Director of Onondaga Savings Bank, relative to a possible opening for a Security Representative position. Mr. Goodfellow advised me that I could file an application for the position, but he thought that someone else might be hired.

Marge's annual vacation was coming up in July of 1982, and we decided to vacation for a week in the New Hampshire area known as Hampton Beach located on the shores of the Atlantic. The week of relaxation went by rapidly. We consumed several freshly boiled lobsters. Marge loved walking the boardwalk with me. The crowds were heavy, and everyone seemed to be enjoying the hot July sun. But as the old saying goes, time waits for no one, so we soon found ourselves back on Sarona Lane in the Town of Clay.

The day after our return home I picked up our mail. To my surprise, two letters, both indicating, "Call me at the Bank," awaited me. They were signed by Mr. Norman M. Goodfellow, Security Director.

When I called Mr. Goodfellow, he asked me if I could come to the Bank the next day for an interview. He informed me that there were other candidates interested in the job, but I would be given equal consideration.

When Marge returned home from the General Electric Company that evening we talked about the call. She seemed happy that I was being considered for the position.

The next morning when I went to Mr. Goodfellow's office, a vice president, Thomas Edson, was also there. I had met Mr. Edson in the Adirondack Mountains several years before, and he remembered me. He and Mr. Goodfellow informed me that I was going to be interviewed by Mr. Richard Callahan, Senior Vice President.

Mr. Callahan was sitting at his desk when I entered his office with his secretary as my escort. Mr. Callahan was wearing a dark blue "power suit." He arose from his desk, excused his secretary, and proceeded to introduce himself to me. He asked me to have a seat, and at this time the interview began.

Vice President Callahan asked many in-depth questions. He delicately probed my background and explained the responsibilities the position required. He told me that I would have to report to two people: Mr. Goodfellow and, in his absence, Mr. Edson. He told me the proposed starting salary and listed the benefits that would accompany the position of Security Representative. He described the size of the Onondaga Savings Bank Organization, covering all departments and their objectives. I felt very relaxed during the interview. Mr. Callahan was most impressive as he continued to explain the banking industry in a most professional fashion.

At the conclusion of the interview he thanked me for making myself available and told me that I would be hearing one way or the other in a few days. We shook hands and I left his office. As I walked down the hallway to the elevator I mused to myself how very different the banking industry was from the semi-military organization to which I had been accustomed.

When I told Marge that evening about my interview with Mr. Callahan, I emphasized that whether or not I was hired for the position I knew one thing for certain: I had met a true gentleman and a true professional with a very keen perception of people.

A few days later I received a telephone call from Mr. Norman M. Goodfellow: my interview with Mr. Callahan was successful, and I was being hired to fill the position of Onondaga Savings Bank new Security Representative. I was very happy with my acceptance into the banking industry in Syracuse, New York.

My duties at the bank consisted of assisting the bank security officer in all bank-related investigations, including the detection of forgery, fraud, and embezzlement violations. To assist all branch managers in matters involving the security of bank assets, including bank employees, bank properties, and to assist the customer base, when called upon to investigate customer related complaints of a criminal nature. And, in the absence of the Security Officer, to assume his duties and report any unusual incidents to the vice president of banking operations.

The next seven years went by very rapidly. My life crossed the paths of thousands of people, from the wealthy elite to the poor street person on the block. The job was a learning experience and it gave me a chance to use my skills in the detection of forgery, fraud, and embezzlement cases, as well as my abilities to relate with co-workers and a large customer base.

Also during this period of time, from 1982 thru 1986 Marge and I entered the State University System of New York via Empire State

College. We both earned Bachelor of Science degrees—my wife in Business Management and I in Community and Human Services. We held our jobs and finished all our coursework over those four years of intense study. College was an experience that we will never forget. The Bank and General Electric allowed us to attend the required residencies at SUNY New Paltz and SUNY Saratoga Springs. We both graduated from the College in 1986. A gala graduation party was held in our honor at the country club in Saratoga Springs. College officials sponsored the graduation event, which was attended by faculty, students, alumni and family members.

Empire College/SUNY offered a unique academic experience based on several different types of programs. Our particular program was known as the "Residency Program," which required interaction with highly educated mentors, experts in their chosen fields of endeavor. The majority of the mentors held doctorate degrees and all held at least a masters' degree.

One of the themes of my studies probed the subject of "Children in Crisis." During my tenure as a police officer I had been involved in many cases where the child was the target of an investigation in which many questions were left unanswered. The questions that haunted me after I closed a juvenile case were "Why did the child exhibit deviant behavior? Was it because he was abused by his parent? Was it because the child was from alcoholic parents? What was the reason? Was it the violence displayed in television programming? Was it because the child came from a poor family? Or a rich family?" So much remained a mystery.

I focused on the child who received a lot of hugs and parental love at birth and on through his stages of development. I sought answers to my haunting questions. To further my inquiry I studied the Psychological and Sociological Theories of Child Abuse, Perspectives of Psychology, Social Institutions, Deviance, and Social Changes, Children In Crisis and the Legal System. I studied the Human Services and how it related to Intervention and Public Policy. I looked at the Alternative Correctional Systems for Children. I read literature and grappled with social change through Literature and Literary Criticism.

I also looked into family case histories and studied juvenile arrest files and juvenile records. I learned that television does have an adverse effect on child behavior by trivializing murder and other criminal activities to a vast audience across our country. I studied the patterns of juvenile criminals in an effort to detect the reasons for such actions.

My extensive investigation revealed that parents who spent the majority of time climbing the social-status ladder without giving proper time to their children were opening the way towards deviant behavior in the future. The child needs nurturing love and devotion from at least one parent, if not both.

The academic adventure of higher learning answered many of my questions about children. It strengthened many of my already established ideologies about people in general. Theory, coupled with my firsthand experience, gave me in-depth insight into the issues of "Children in Crisis."

In the fall of 1987 I began my Masters Degree work in "Culture and Policy" studies through Empire State College/ SUNY.

Along with our studies, Marge and I participated in many social functions during my tenure with OnBank. In addition we became involved in a Bank-sponsored art course, pursuing the mediums of pastels, oil painting and water color. The course was held in-house at the Bank on Tuesday evenings for ten to twelve students, under the direction of a local artist, an employee of Onondaga Savings Bank. This course enhanced our perceptions, and made us more aware of art objects, and raised our interest in Art in general. We painted objects of our choice as our teacher threaded useful theory into our class instructions. We entered our completed works into the "On Your Own Time" Program once a year. We took the course for four years. Our work was displayed in the main lobby of Onondaga Savings Bank for two to four weeks before being graded by professional artists. Those judged best would then be displayed in the Syracuse Everson Museum. Although neither Marge nor I reached the ultimate showing in Everson, we both gained a great amount of appreciation for creativity.

As I continue my reflections about my bank experience, I am happy to say I learned a great deal from all the working staff. Many of the young people were the age of our children. I was very impressed with their eagerness to pursue their work objectives. The bank in turn awarded the efforts of its employees and instilled in them the importance of education as it applied to their needs in the work environment. In addition, the

Bank's association with AIB (American Institute of Banking) furthered many employees towards their goals by assisting them with tuition payment when the employee participated in AIB Courses.

Upon the completion of seven years with the bank, and as I reached the magic age of sixty, I opted to take an early retirement. This was a difficult choice for me to make, and sometimes I could kick myself in the breeches for retiring from the bank: however I was inspired to retire as Marge retired from the General Electric Company in 1989. Both of us could have worked longer in our careers, but we felt that the time was right to make the decision we did.

During my times of reflection I have often thought about the fact that it is alright to do your job well in whatever profession you pursue. It isn't alright to choose the career without considering your priorities. The family has to come first, after God, and only then your career.

Since 1989, we have traveled the United States, Canada and Mexico in our motor home. We have a beautiful country and we met many great Americans along our path. Our neighbors to the north and to the south were most gracious to us. We have visited many interesting places in our journey including museums, historical buildings, national parks and other places of interest.

In 1993 my first wife, Peggy passed away. In 1994, while in Arizona, our golden labrador retriever, "Crackers" (born on the 4th of July) died at age 15. In 1995, my mother, my queen, Marjorie Ann Briant nee Timmerman, passed away at 91. My sons are married and reside with their families in the New England area.

Even though my life has had its valleys and peaks, I have been a most fortunate person to have survived the hostilities of many people who never took time in their life to know me, not as a competitor, but as a person. I have finally been able to share my life with someone who unselfishly took time to care and understand what a cop goes through, a cop who gave so much of his life to the strangers he served.